It Happened, It's Over, It's OK Now!

How to Let Go of the Past and Heal Your Mind, Memory and Emotions

Barbara Brown, MSE
Dr. Tom Taylor

It Happened, It's Over, It's OK Now!
How to Let Go of the Past
and Heal Your Mind, Memory and Emotions

Cover Design: Sammy Blindell, www.HowToBuildaBrand.org

ISBN: 978-1-929921-44-7 (PREMIUM EDITION)
978-1-929921-47-8 (Regular Edition)
978-1-929921-45-4 (E-Book)

Published and Produced in the U.S.A. by

Divine Health is Your Original Design

www.**WholeLifeWholeHealth**.com

201 S. Shady Shores Dr., #1952 • Lake Dallas, TX 75065 • 940-725-0023

The information contained in this work is based upon the research, personal and professional experience of the authors and other health care professionals who contributed to this body of knowledge. It is not intended to diagnose or treat any illness, or as a substitute for consulting with your health care provider.

It Happened,
It's Over,
It's OK Now!

Dedication

To the Creator of us all:

Thank You for the keys to restore Divine Health to Your creation.

"If you listen carefully to the Lord your God and do what is right in His eyes, if you pay attention to His commands and keep all His decrees, I will not bring on you any of the diseases I brought on the Egyptians, for I am the Lord, Who heals you." (Exodus 15:26, NIV)

"If you pay attention to these laws and are careful to follow them, then the Lord your God will keep His covenant of love with you ... The Lord will keep you free from every disease."
(Deuteronomy 7:12, 15, NIV)

"See, I have set before you today life and prosperity, and death and adversity; in that I command you today to love the Lord your God, to walk in His ways and to keep His commandments and His statutes and His judgments, that you may live and multiply, and that the Lord your God may bless you in the land where you are entering to possess it." (Deuteronomy 30:15-16, NASB)

Foreword

As a family physician who practiced medicine in four countries on three continents, I have seen the impact of illness and disease on tens of thousands of individuals and their families over the course of my career. The principles in this book can change the outcome for infants in South India dying of dysentery, Romanian orphans with severe asthma, or middle-aged American women just diagnosed with breast cancer.

Even though I thought I had "gotten over" caring for my mother and losing her to Multiple Sclerosis when I was 16 years-old, I learned that healing can occur in layers. When I attended a workshop in 2010 led by Barbara Brown, MSE, and Dr. Tom Taylor, I felt relieved that someone finally understood what I was still silently working through and could help me win the victory. At the same time, I felt the training upon which I hung my proverbial hat challenged to the core.

The emotional memory cleansing process in this book has revolutionized my life. It has also dramatically changed how I approach patients, family, friends and even the cashier at the grocery store. Now, instead of getting hurt or offended, I ask, *"What can I learn from this encounter?"*

People's personalities and lives are the result of their accumulated experiences and what they've seen modeled in front of them. Their behaviors today are probably the best they can do.

Barbara often says, *"We are each where our choices have led us."*

Dr. Taylor says, *"If you don't like where you are, you have only two choices: Change your location, or change how you see your location."*

Well, that certainly eliminates all the excuses.

What if there have been no mistakes? What if nothing has merely happened *to* me, but rather, *for* me? Only one letter separates "bitter" from "better," and I can choose whether to become bitter or better as a result of any experience in my life.

Despite many years of hearing Romans 8:28, the words and the promise are more precious now than ever before:

> **"We know that God causes all things to work together for good to those who love God, to those who are called according to His purpose."** (NASB)

Even if I'm uncomfortable right now and I wish things were different, I can trust that my Heavenly Father has written this into my life story for a specific purpose.

> **"Your eyes saw my embryo, and my days, all of them were written upon Your scroll; the days, they were formed when there was not one of them."**
> (Psalm 139:16, CLV)

As Barbara says, *"God is very efficient. He's always working on more than one person at a time,"* so instead of asking, *"Why me?"* ask, *"What do I need to learn here?"*

I stepped down from a thriving family medicine practice to work with Barbara and Dr. Taylor at Whole Life Whole Health, because I believe that getting their life-saving and health-enhancing procedures, protocols, and products to the world is so critical.

Everyone I've ever met would benefit from this book and I pray that you *apply* what you learn in the pages that follow. When you do, it will change your life. It has radically changed mine and the lives of so many whom I've had the privilege to know, love and serve.

Claudia Gabrielle, MD, FAAFP

Table of Contents

Introduction

Since 1990, Barbara Brown and I have seen thousands of lives changed and conditions healed when others had given up hope, using the principles you'll find in this book. We've observed that healing is an inevitable outcome when interference from its natural expression is identified and removed.

We discovered that merging science and Scripture provides a *complete* understanding of sickness and healing, demonstrating how your body works in concert with your spirit and mind (or soul). Scientific principles make well-living logical and understandable; scriptural principles make life itself meaningful. Science explains *"how it works"*; Scripture explains *"why it works."* You'll find lots of references to both in this book.

If you had been the architect of your life, you may have left some situations or relationships out of the plan, or written others in. If you had your life to live again, you'd make other choices, but that isn't going to happen, and the fact is, you are today precisely where your choices have led you.

In our title, *"It Happened"* simply acknowledges the events and people we've encountered throughout our lives. This may seem obvious, but we've worked with people who preferred to imagine that a situation or relationship never happened at all, even though their denial was creating physical illness. To the degree that someone refuses to acknowledge that an event or relationship could have caused a problem, healing cannot happen, because the person's survival mechanism will forever be preoccupied trying to run from or fight with an unwanted memory. At some point, one or more systems in the body will become exhausted and a form of illness, disease, or dysfunction is the inevitable outcome.

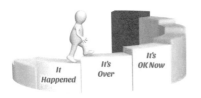

There is no escaping the truth and your spirit *knows* the truth. Your body only responds to what your spirit knows is true, so for healing to occur, acknowledging *"It Happened"* is the first step to take.

"It's Over" simply recognizes that we aren't bound to continue or repeat the situations, circumstances, or relationships we acknowledge. Instead, we're free to look for the real *source* of whatever ails us.

> You can't change or "un-live" an event that happened 50 years ago or five minutes ago. They're both over and healing is waiting for you here and now.

Of course, the exception to this rule is a currently ongoing event or relationship. Not to worry; it's still possible to change what you think, feel, and believe about it, so healing can progress. We'll deal with this in the chapters to come.

"It's OK Now" is a statement recognizing that we don't have to be victims of anything that happened and is over (or is ongoing). We can even learn how to make the worst experiences we can remember *"OK Now."*

You'll know you've succeeded when you're actually glad for what has happened in your life. All the experiences that brought you here are worth it, because of who you are today, how far you've come, and the "jewels" in your life that you wouldn't trade for anything.

You are not an accident of creation and your life isn't a series of lucky steps, terrible mistakes, and near misses. Your Creator knew exactly where you'd be today and all the steps it would take to bring you to this page now.

> *"For all my ways You have made provision."* (Psalm 139:3, CLV)

God didn't make your choices *for* you or drag you into them. He did, however, know what choices you'd make and His plan for you provided for each one.

Psalm 139:16 is even more specific:

"And my days, all of them were written upon Your scroll; the days, they were formed when there was not one of them." (CLV)

In his book, *Learned Optimism*, psychologist, Martin Seligman, wrote that humans *believe* that what they think is *true*, simply because they *think* it. What you think or believe may not be true at all, but what *is* true remains true no matter what you think or believe.

Well, believe this:

> **You were created by a loving God and, like a friend said,**
> *"God doesn't make junk!"*

Recognizing the "sovereignty of God" provides an unshakable foundation of knowledge, understanding and wisdom that brings clarity, certainty and peace to your soul. Here's what the sovereignty of God means:

"God … is operating all in all" (1 Corinthians 12:6, CLNT). In other words, God is running everything everywhere. He has always been in charge and He is right now. He is ultimately responsible for

everything that has gone on in the world or that goes on today. He isn't in Heaven wringing His hands wondering what's gone wrong with His creation. He knew everything that would occur in your life and He let it happen, so any "beef" you have is ultimately with Him.

Understanding the sovereignty of God, or at least allowing for it, helps explain the course your life has taken so far; how you got where you are today; why even your "free will" does not escape God's sovereignty; why there have been no accidents, even though you may think you've made some terrible mistakes.

A world renowned doctor once told Barbara and me, *"Whatever your condition is, you earned it. Blaming others, the weather, genetics, or Aunt Mildred's spoiled cheese casserole won't cut it. You did something, said something (or didn't, or couldn't for whatever reason), thought something, judged someone, ate something you shouldn't have … and whatever followed, you earned it."*

"But what about babies born with no brains or terribly deformed?" God knows who they are and what their purpose is, or was, for living.

When I showed up at Dr. Daryl Rhoades' office in Topeka, Kansas, after several weeks of waking at night with a completely numb left arm, I had no idea that I had earned my condition, but something was clearly not right.

That first appointment opened up a new paradigm of health care that I didn't know existed and the experience altered my life.

My symptoms resolved within three weeks and I discovered a new awareness of how my body felt that scared me a little at first. I felt soreness at the base of my neck one day while driving to work. "Where did that come from?" I wondered. "Was my work with Dr. Rhoades actually hurting me rather than helping? I never had this happen before. Maybe I should never have started down this road."

Suddenly, I realized that I had probably ignored a lot of how I felt before, but now I was acquiring a new level of body awareness. My initial feeling of alarm changed to empowered.

The new sensations I felt were *signals* that a change was needed; maybe as simple as adjusting my posture. I shifted my position and the soreness stopped! I repeated the process over and over. I began to be excited by *any* sensation I felt in my body, and even more excited when a change I made resolved it.

When I told Dr. Rhoades about this, he said, "You might want to learn about the 'mind-body' connection." Over the next hour, he demonstrated how my body responded to my thoughts, feelings and beliefs. Even more important was the revelation that my body responded positively to true statements and negatively to false ones. The responses were clear, instantaneous, and could not be faked or fooled.

I spent the next day realizing that I was creating my physical, mental and emotional state, moment-by-moment, by what I *thought* about and how I *felt* about what I thought about.

When a car was "hogging" the passing lane on my way to work, I began feeling irritated, frustrated and headed toward anger when my awareness kicked in. All day, I connected how I felt physically with my thoughts and emotions.

I realized that all of us are creating our state of physical, mental and emotional health by what we think and feel throughout our days, and that the effects accumulate in physical symptoms. If the cycle continues, we create real illness, but, because we don't recognize our role in this process, we run for the nearest remedy. The cycle continues until we find ourselves in even bigger trouble.

Follow this progression from feeling symptoms to identifying the cause:

- Why did I lose feeling in my arm?
  - A nerve bundle traveling through my neck was compressed.
- Why were my nerves being compressed?
  - My spine had straightened abnormally.
- Why did my spine straighten?
  - My muscles tightened as if I was in a constant battle.
- Why was I in a constant battle?
  - Mental and emotional stress at work and at home combined with poor posture over a period of years.
- Finally, the symptoms drove me to seek help, and they resolved in less than a month.
- I sat differently at work and slept on a pillow that supported the natural curve in my neck.
- More importantly, I learned to recognize how my thoughts, feelings and beliefs affected my body; how to break those patterns and reverse their effects, or prevent them.

The process of moving from *"It Happened,"* through *"It's Over,"* to *"It's OK Now,"* took about three months for me. While the progression above was going on, I also began learning how to help others go their own processes.

Other experiences have taken as long as 10 years to heal. The length of time is less important than the harmony created between your spirit, mind, and body along the way.

Here's how it works in a nutshell:

A feeling of *"dis-ease"* leads to symptoms that can lead to a disease, which leads to a diagnosis, which leads to a treatment, which masks the symptoms; but the original *dis-ease* continues, which leads to new symptoms ... and the cycle continues until you address the original *dis-ease.*

In our experience, situations, circumstances and relationships that we wish hadn't happened are designed by God to bring us to the end of ourselves, so that all we have left is to come to Him. These events are evidence of God's love and purpose for us, not His neglect or displeasure; they are evidence of our worth, not our worthlessness. Through our worst experiences, He risks our total rejection of Him to bring us to Himself.

Within God's sovereignty, there are no mistakes, only lessons. Situations and relationships don't happen *TO* you, as if you're bouncing from one mistake to the next. The truth is, everything happens *FOR* you to learn from and to bring you closer to your Creator Who loves you and wants a relationship with you.

Jesus wasn't any happier about facing crucifixion than we are to deal with our own "issues." He went through far worse than you or I can imagine and came out triumphant. Ask for His help prayerfully and expect to walk through whatever you face; maybe not perfectly in every step, but successfully in the end.

Dr. Tom Taylor

Take advantage of the online resources for this book at
ItsOK.WholeLifeWholeHealth.com

Chapter 1

Who's Driving Your Car?

And whose voice is in your GPS?

We all want to be happy.

We want to be in the "driver's seat" of our lives. We want to be in control of ourselves and, as far as it's possible, our surroundings – our environment.

In my last corporate job, the first thing I did in my office was to disconnect the fluorescent light bulbs, and bring in a floor lamp and a desk lamp, because I found the warm incandescent light more relaxing and it was easier to concentrate.

Who doesn't dress up their work space to make it their own? For that matter, don't we make all the spaces we live and work in more comfortable, if only emotionally, by decorating or furnishing them in ways that make us feel good?

Why? We want to be happy.

> Abraham Lincoln said, *"Most people are about as happy as they want to be."*

The key word in Lincoln's quotation is "*want,*" which is a nice way of saying that even the grumpiest person, who seems to find fault with almost everyone and everything, is as happy as he or she *wants* to be, or is *choosing* to be.

Dr. Barry Neil Kaufman, author of, *Happiness is a Choice*, had firsthand experience with this subject: He and his wife raised a severely autistic child by entering his world, instead of requiring him to fit into theirs. It worked, too, because their son is now an accomplished author and lecturer.

Today, Kaufman's "Options Institute" is focused on helping people find happiness by changing their perspectives.

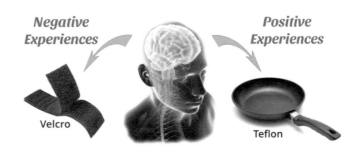

In his book, *Hardwiring Happiness*, Rick Hanson states, *"Your brain is like Velcro for negative experiences but Teflon for positive ones."* In other words, we remember longer and more vividly the experiences, situations, and relationships that we wish had been different or wish hadn't happened at all, instead of our child's first smile.

What does all this have to do with physical health?

Your immune system responds to your level of happiness and the happier you are, the healthier you are. The science of psychoneuroimmunology is built around investigating and demonstrating how the so-called, *"Mind-Body Connection"* – which Barbara Brown and I more appropriately call, the *"Spirit-Mind-Body Connection"* – works in the mind, or psyche; the nervous and immune systems.

Dr. Candace Pert, author of *The Molecules of Emotion,* called by some, *"the mother of psychoneuroimmunology,"* said this:

"We've all heard about Psychosomatic Illness, but have you heard about Psychosomatic Wellness? Since emotions run every system in the body, don't underestimate their power to treat and heal."

Researchers now know that emotions, such as loneliness, worry, and anxiety produce chemicals that lower the efficiency of your immune system. They not only make you susceptible to illness, but they allow latent viruses like Epstein-Barr to reactivate,

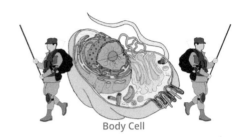

Body Cell

systemic inflammation to run amuck, cause tissue damage, and increase your risk of chronic diseases such as atherosclerosis (hardening and narrowing of the arteries), cancer and diabetes.

The good news is that emotions like happiness also produce chemicals that reinforce your immune system and reverse the damage that negative emotions cause. The more delighted you feel about every aspect of your life, the

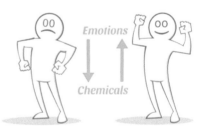

greater the benefit to your physical health and your sense of well-being.

Soon after medical science decided that genetics determines everything, scientists like Dr. Steve Cole at UCLA and Dr. Bruce Lipton, author of *The Biology of Belief* and a pioneer in the growing field of epigenetics, have demonstrated that your genes change according to your *thoughts* and *emotions*.

Dr. Edward Bach, the British physician and founder of the Flower Essence Society, said human beings need two things to thrive:

1. **A sense of purpose or meaning**
2. **The ability to express and receive love**

Are both of these present in your life?

Barbara Brown and I have worked with people in the ministry and the wellness field, respectively, since 1990, and our discoveries parallel those made by the scientists mentioned above, among many others. More importantly, though, the processes we present in this book enable you to recognize your physical, mental, emotional, and even spiritual states; shed what no longer serves you; and develop and strengthen what causes joy to spring from inside you. This is the actual definition of "happy" in ancient, biblical Greek.

> **HAPPY:**
> *Joyousness springing from within*

The apostle Paul wrote in his first letter to his protégé, Timothy, ***"In accord with the evangel [gospel] of the glory of the happy God, with which I was entrusted"*** (1 Timothy 1:11, CLNT).

Think of it: *"The happy God,"* a God with joy springing from within Himself!

Well, if He created us in His image, then it follows that you and I are capable of exactly the same *"joyousness springing from within"* ourselves.

- Wouldn't we be better off if we experienced this every day we're alive?
- What would our relationships look like?
- How might our perspectives change for the better at work and at home?
- How might our health and well-being improve in ways and in areas we may not have imagined possible?

"Pastor Will Bowen of Christ Church Unity in Kansas City knows well the power of changing the way you think. In an effort to help his congregation find a concrete way to focus on what they do want rather than what they don't want, he created a purple bracelet and gave one to everyone at church one Sunday. Because it takes 21 days to create a new habit, the idea was for people to switch the bracelet to the other wrist if they found themselves complaining (one of the most common forms of negative thinking)—and keep switching it until they'd gone the full 21 days without a single complaint.

"The 'Complaint-Free World' project exploded from 250 bracelets to five million in nine months. Pastor Will receives letters daily from schools, prisons, hospitals, churches, businesses, even the Pentagon, telling him what a powerful and positive impact the bracelets are having. Families are getting closer. People's health is improving. People are turning their lives around." (Jennifer Read Hawthorne, author of *Change Your Thoughts, Change Your World*, © 2014)

"Thoughts are things," and *"What you think about, you bring about,"* were phrases we often heard in seminars that we attended throughout the 1990's and early 2000's. We were delighted when Japanese scientist, Dr. Masaru Emoto, published photographs of frozen water molecules that were subjected to various thoughts, emotions, and music. The snowflake-like patterns were either stunningly beautiful or pathetically distorted, depending on the energetic frequencies that different thoughts, emotions, or music created. Even terribly polluted water changed its patterns when prayer was introduced!

BEFORE PRAYER.........AFTER PRAYER

> What if your own body, which is made up of at least 70 percent water, is just as affected by the energy frequencies of your thoughts, feelings and beliefs? Would you be bathing in a crystal clear lake, or a toxic waste site?

Try writing down at least one negative thought about yourself or your life every day for a week. Then, apply the *"Heart, Soul and Spirit Cleanse"* that you'll find later in this book. We predict that you'll learn a great deal about why you feel the way you do most of the time; but even more importantly, you'll learn how to change your patterns and heal your mind, memory and emotions. The side effects will be a healthier body and a happier life!

> If you hear a little voice inside, saying, *"This is going to take a lot work to break out of these cycles,"* there's your first negative thought to record.

Where do negative beliefs like the one above come from? Who told you so? What voice(s) have you been listening to and why is the focus on how *hard* things might be?

Think about how often you think about what you don't like, don't want, or don't have. And, if not you, you probably know someone who frequently complains about what they don't like, don't want, or don't have.

What would happen if we focused on what we *DO* like, *DO* want, *DO* have, and how easy things could be?

How do we do that? What if we changed the voice(s) inside our heads? The answer is a simple scriptural principle, but it's so simple that most people dismiss it without a second thought, even though it works 100 percent of the time:

> *"In everything be giving thanks, for this is the will of God in Christ Jesus for you."* (1 Thessalonians 5:18, CLNT)

In one of her articles, author, Jennifer Read Hawthorne writes, *"It's impossible NOT to make a difference in the world around you. The only question is, what kind of difference do you want to make? What you radiate to the world through who you are is far more significant than anything you do."*

One of what Barbara Brown and I call the *"Eight Master Keys"* is, *"What You SPEAK."* You know how powerful words are from your own experiences growing up. Kids are likely to believe the voices of authority figures they respect when they're told that they will amount to nothing. These kids are going to fight upstream against that belief for most of their lives, if they fight it at all. Fortunately, the opposite is also true, and hopefully you are one of those success stories.

Our recommendation is simple, *"Watch your mouth,"* and pay attention to this practical scriptural principle:

> *"Do not be quick with your mouth, do not be hasty in your heart to utter anything before God ... Why should God be angry at what you say and destroy the work of your hands?"* (Ecclesiastes 5:2,6, NIV)

While we're on the subject, we should add, *"Watch your ears."* Jesus said, **"Beware what you are hearing!"** (Mark 4:24, CLNT). In other words, protect yourself from the literal poison that can come through the voices of others.

The voice(s) you listen to can act kind of like a GPS. The problem is that you can bless or curse with a word and, just as easily, you can be blessed or cursed with a word.

My mother frequently reminded my sisters and me of a popular takeaway line from the animated Disney feature, "Bambi," when Thumper, the rabbit, says, *"If you can't say somethin' nice, don't say nothin' at all."*

> **Never "own" an illness; never say, *"My diabetes,"* etc.**
> **You can say what you *have*, or you can *have* what you *say*.**

Diagnosis and prognosis are two of the worst services that doctors perform, because the words often become terribly limiting.

> A physician's *diagnosis* is a conclusion based on training, and they can only treat what they can diagnose.
> A physician's *prognosis* is a prediction based on his or her experience and that of others in the field.

Diagnoses and prognoses are often wrong and they are not conducive to healing. Just because your body demonstrates a condition that can be assigned a name and a "usual" outcome, you aren't bound to the belief system that surrounds it.

Go free from the myth of "authority," and don't accept someone else's prediction or pronouncement. Adopt a, *"Who says so?"* attitude. After all, who is the final authority on you and on what is true? Your *Creator's* voice is the only truly accurate GPS. What does God say about you?

Here are only three out of hundreds of examples:

> *"The Father Himself is fond of you, seeing that you are fond of Me, and have believed that I came out from God."* (John 16:27, CLNT)

> *"Thus says the Lord ... I have loved you with an everlasting love; therefore I have drawn you with lovingkindness."* (Jeremiah 31:2-3, NASB)
>
> *"The love of God has been poured out in our hearts through the Holy Spirit which is being given to us."* (Romans 5:5, CLNT)

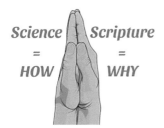

Science = **HOW**   *Scripture* = **WHY**

When you contemplate Scriptures like the ones above, you'll find that science and Scripture are entirely compatible with one another. Science explains *how* we work. Scriptures provide insight into *why* we work the way we do, and instructions to help us work better, realize our potential, and fulfill our purpose.

Barbara's miraculous healing from muscular dystrophy is a testimony of receiving what God says rather than taking on a medical prognosis. What follows is an excerpt from the first chapter of her book, *GOD is GOD and We Are Not.*

JERRY, CRIPPLES DO WALK!

Monday was "flat-on-my-back" time after another grueling week and a full day of church on Sunday. All of my muscles were exhausted...again. My legs wouldn't work, my neck wouldn't hold my head up, and my hands wouldn't grip. Nothing worked. The condition I didn't want to acknowledge was getting worse.

Lying in bed, I prayed, *"God, I know You've called me to be a missionary, but how can I do it flat on my back?"* (Women in the denomination I was in at the time could either tend the nursery at church, or go to Africa as missionaries.) Finally, I prayed a prayer God could answer, because my heart was to build His kingdom rather than mine.

I had become progressively weaker over the previous five years. The doctors at the Muscular Dystrophy Clinic in Little Rock charted my decline by performing painful biopsies, shocking my nerve endings with electrodes, and carrying out other tests to see how much muscle I had left.

The diagnosis was Charcot-Marie-Tooth, the same diagnosis my dad had received 33 years earlier. The doctors warned my family that CMT, a disease that causes progressive and severe muscle atrophy, was inherited and that two of Daddy's four kids would get it. The prognosis was grim at best.

I had sponsored MDA "Love Runs" for years through my athletic stores and appeared on the Jerry Lewis Telethons, raising money for the Muscular Dystrophy Association to find a cure. With no hope in sight, I was desperate.

"Someone HAS to know more," I told my doctor. *"Where are the answers?"* It wasn't okay with me to be crippled at only 35 years old. I had a life to live and my body needed to "line up." My last resort was to go to the MDA Research Center at Columbia Presbyterian Medical Center in New York City. Two weeks later, the doctor there confirmed the diagnosis I had dreaded.

"The tests are complete and they're all positive. You have Charcot-Marie-Tooth," the doctor said as he finished his analysis. *"You know the progression of the disease. There's no treatment; there's no cure."* I knew it well. From the time I was a child, I watched both my dad and my aunt wither away with the disease.

While the doctor was speaking, suddenly, JESUS APPEARED! I had no idea He made "house calls." I wanted to ask the doctor, *"Do you have a clue Who's here?"* There was nothing in my data bank to prepare me for such a visitation. Jesus looked down at me and said, *"Barbara! When are you just going to trust Me?"*

There was such life in His words that I stood up and declared to the doctor, *"God's going to heal me! I'm going home. No more tests."*

The doctor looked at me and laughed. I checked out of the hotel, headed back to Arkansas, and told my doctors there the same thing: *"God's going to heal me! No more tests."* They laughed too.

I had never experienced a vision before. No one told me

"those things" still happened; you know, the "stuff" the first Apostles did. (Read Acts 2:17-21, 10:3-17 and 16:9-10) But I had seen the Lord! His words were clear and I knew by the spirit that God would heal me, so I spoke that declaration by faith.

> *"Death and life are in the power of the tongue, and those who love it will eat its fruit."* (Proverbs 18:21, NASB)

One day, weeks after my declaration to the doctors in Arkansas, the Lord said, *"Start walking!"*

"God, this is killing me!" I replied.

He said, *"You're dying anyway; just do what I said."*

We're all dying anyway, aren't we? Why don't we just do what He says?

I believe we all have crippled places in our lives that God wants to heal; some are just more obvious than others.

I began taking one painful step at a time...then five steps...then ten. I started walking. At times, I was sure it would kill me. I walked, and walked, and walked.

Thirty days later, I RAN all the way home HEALED. Praise God!

I called Jerry Lewis to tell him I wouldn't be on the telethon again, because, *"By Jesus' wounds, I'm healed."* (Read Isaiah 53:5 and I Peter 2:24)

Are you wondering about this *"God speaking to me"* stuff? Remember, Jesus said, **"My sheep hear My voice, and I know them, and they follow Me"** (John 10:27, NASB).

The Apostle Paul wrote about the gifts of the Holy Spirit:

> *"There are varieties of effects, but the same God Who works all things in all persons. But to each one is given the manifestation of the Spirit for the common good. For to one is given the word of wisdom through the Spirit, and to another the word of knowledge according to the same Spirit; to another faith by the same Spirit, and to another gifts of healing by the one Spirit, and to another the effecting of miracles, and to another prophecy, and to another the distinguishing of spirits, to another various kinds of tongues, and to another the interpretation of tongues. But one and the same*

> *Spirit works all these things, distributing to each one individually just as He wills."*
> (1 Corinthians 12:6-11, NASB)

My healing was the "working out" of a miracle. I had to do my part; then God did His.

Before the Lord miraculously healed me, I couldn't go beyond where my withering muscles would take me and what little hope remained.

Suddenly, I had to reevaluate everything about my life. I had come face to face with a God so big that the word He spoke activated my faith. Now it was up to me to LIVE my faith, like the Bible says, **"the righteous man shall live by faith"** (Habakkuk 2:4, Romans 1:17, NASB).

> *"Without faith it is impossible to please Him, for he who comes to God must believe that He is and that He is a rewarder of those who seek Him."* (Hebrews 11:6, NASB)

> *"He said to her, 'Daughter, your faith has made you well; go in peace, and be healed of your affliction.'"* (Mark 5:34, NASB)

> *"Jesus said to him, 'Go; your faith has made you well.' Immediately he regained his sight and began following Him on the road."* (Mark 10:52, NASB)

> *"When the Son of Man comes, will He find faith on the Earth?"* (Luke 18:8, NASB)

> *"Whatever is not from faith is sin."* (Romans 14:23, NASB)

Do you know the walk of faith? Do you know what the word of God is over YOUR life? You'll find the answers in the Scriptures, between Genesis and Revelation.

> *"So will My word be which goes forth from My mouth; it will not return to Me empty, without accomplishing what I desire, and without succeeding in the matter for which I sent it."* (Isaiah 55:11, NASB)

Jesus said, **"Heaven and Earth will pass away, but My words will not pass away"** (Matthew 24:35, NASB).

Who is speaking the word of God over your life?

When muscular dystrophy was ravaging my body, my friend Joyce always said, *"Barbara, I'm praying for you and God's going to heal you."*

I responded to her the same way every time: *"Joyce, I told you, this is inherited and two of us four kids are supposed to get it; I'm just the first."*

Joyce always declared, *"The Bible says that by Jesus' stripes we ARE healed, and I'm not going to quit praying."*

Years later, as I was planning a trip that would include a stop in Little Rock, I prayed, *"God, I would love to see Joyce again and show her I'm healed."*

I went to my favorite store on my way through Little Rock; a large department store with two floors. I knew exactly where to go, so it wouldn't take long to run in, get what I needed, and run out. As I was leaving with my purchase, I spotted Joyce. In a 30-second window of time, our paths miraculously crossed.

"Joyce, look, I'm healed!"

She said, *"I never quit praying."*

I'm STILL walking, years later, on Joyce's prayers. Praise God! Today, no one in my family has muscular dystrophy, nor will they. The generational curse is broken and we have escaped.

Who's walking on *your* prayers? Who are you believing for who doesn't have faith to believe for themselves?

In the next chapter, we'll discuss what it takes to unlock your imagination and remove limitations you may not have known that you've placed on yourself.

Nutshells and Takeaways from Chapter 1

- Your immune system responds to your level of happiness and the happier you are, the healthier you are.

- Happy means, "Joyousness springing from within."

- *"In everything be giving thanks, for this is the will of God in Christ Jesus for you."*
  (1 Thessalonians 5:18, CLNT)

- Watch your mouth. You can bless or curse with a word.

- Never "own" an illness. You can *say* what you *have*, or you can *have* what you *say*.

- A physician's *diagnosis* is a conclusion based on training. A *prognosis* is a prediction based on experience.

- Adopt a, *"Who says so?"* attitude.

- Science and Scripture are entirely compatible with one another.

- Science explains *how* we work. Scriptures provide insight into *why* we work the way we do, plus instructions to help us work better, realize our potential, and fulfill our purpose.

- Jesus looked down at me and said, *"When are you just going to trust Me?"*

- He said, *"You're dying anyway; just do what I said."* We're all dying anyway, aren't we? Why don't we just do what He says?

- We all have crippled places in our lives that God wants to heal; some are just more obvious than others.

- Barbara's healing was the "working out" of a miracle. She had to do her part; then God did His.

Chapter 2

How to Unlock Your Imagination and Remove Limitations
The power of asking questions

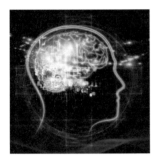

We are always thinking. That's what our brains do. Even if we say we aren't thinking anything, the truth is, we're always thinking something.

Strangely, as much as 98 percent of your thoughts today are identical to the ones you had yesterday and the day before. Unless something dramatic changes, 98 percent of your thoughts today will be the same ones tomorrow and the day after.

But here's what's troubling:

> **80% of all our thoughts are negative.**

Bestselling author and speaker, Jennifer Read Hawthorne, must have read the same Stanford University study on human thinking that I read back in the 1990's. Ms. Hawthorne, however, left out the scariest statistic of the whole study:

> **60% of the 80% of our negative thoughts today are self-referring. In other words, almost half of all our thinking is not only negative, but it's negative about ourselves and our lives!**

It's no wonder that we regularly get ourselves wound up, mentally, emotionally … and ultimately even physically.

There's a fast way to *change* your thinking. You can do it right now and it's so simple that you won't even have to write it down. You might want to anyway, because it'll help you often … if you use it.

ASK QUESTIONS.

Instead of drawing conclusions, forming opinions, or, worst of all, making judgments, ASK QUESTIONS. In fact, ask one *specific* question, and when you ask it, *keep* asking it until it becomes a game, because the best part is, you never have to *answer* the question … you only have to  *ask* it. Your brain, which is THE best problem-solving / question-answering organ ever created, will go on a relentless search for answers, and it will present you with possibilities that you never imagined before.

Barbara Brown and I have presented this powerful questioning tool in various seminars and videos, but too many people ignore it, or worse, dismiss it:

> The question is, *"What if _____?"* (fill in the blank),
> and follow that up with, *"What would that look like?"*

If you haven't seen the video of the day a colleague and I bent a six-foot section of steel rebar that was placed against our throats, you should watch it (it's part of the online resource that goes with this book).

Here's an example of applying the "what if" question to the notion of bending rebar the way my colleague and I did in front of 1,000 people (The video can be seen at ItsOK.WholeLifeWholeHealth.com):

- Bending rebar between your hands *might* be possible, but not with your throats!
- *Yeah, but what if it were possible? What would that look like?*
- Well, OK, but that would take a lot of strength and your throat is so soft!
- *Yeah, but what if it were possible? What would that look like?*
- OK, but rebar is really stiff and besides, the end of it would hurt your throat – maybe even puncture it.
- *Yeah, but what if it were possible? What would that look like?*

You get the idea, right? Asking *"what if"* is a like kid's game, and your brain loves games, and we love being kids, after all, don't we?

Now, lest you think this is a bit simplistic and can't possibly work, ask yourself, *"What if it's entirely possible to shift my thinking just by asking a question? What would that look like?"*

> **Remember, you only have to *ask* the question.**
> **Answers will arrive all on their own.**

I was once invited to participate in a kind of boot camp for speakers and trainers. I'd already taken time out of my busy office several times that year, so I told the guy who had invited me that there was no way I could take that time off.

All he said was, "Are you sure?"

Even though I had already made my decision, I decided to try the "what if" game, and less than 24 hours later, a whole plan appeared. In a few weeks, I was in the boot camp among outstanding trainers and coaches, and the experience did wonders for my effectiveness as a speaker and trainer.

Asking questions inside himself is exactly how Albert Einstein performed his famous *"thought experiments"* and arrived at his theory of general relativity. Christopher Columbus considered the radical notion of a round world by asking questions that challenged the conventional wisdom of his time.

Asking questions engages our imaginations in a constructive way that turns fanciful notions into reality. Imagination put us on pirate ships and battle fields as boys, or into elaborate, full-dress weddings and formal tea parties when my sisters were little girls.

We didn't *have* to ask questions when we played as children, because there were no limits to our imaginations and *everything* was possible. What if there are no limits to your imagination today, and everything is still possible? What would that look like?

When we grew up in the 50's and 60's, the phrase, *"Made in Japan"* used to mean anything junky or cheap – something like a transistor radio or toaster. That all changed over a period of 20 years or so, but back then you could plan on the product breaking and eventually throwing it out.

You weren't *"Made in Japan."* You aren't junk. **You were created perfectly by God and He doesn't make junk.** Your body is performing exactly according to His original blueprint that resides in you from the moment of conception.

What if you are perfect right now, just the way you are? Even if your body hurts somewhere, or an illness has a hold on you, what if you're perfect already? What would that look like?

Even when it might seem like you're falling apart, all that's happening is that the expression of your divine blueprint got covered up with debris,* like the floor of your garage. All that's needed is a good clearing out and sweeping off, and your original design will express itself exactly as God created it.

* *"Debris"* consists of less than ideal choices in the areas of the *"8 Master Keys that Unlock Your Total Health."* You'll find a link to these on this book's online resource page, but here's a list of them:

- What you EAT
- What you DRINK
- What and How you BREATHE
- How you EXERCISE (or don't!)
- How you REST
- What you THINK, FEEL, and BELIEVE
- What you SPEAK
- How you NURTURE YOUR SPIRIT

The better choices you make in the eight areas listed above, the easier it is for your original blueprint to express itself!

What if robust health and feeling great in every area of your life is just that simple? What would that look like?

What if you made just one small change in one small area today, and another tomorrow, and so on … What would that look like in 30 days … 60 … 90?

Keep asking "What if..." questions and share your insights on the Whole Life Whole Health Facebook Group.

In the next chapter, we'll address your level of happiness and how to get more of it.

 ## Nutshells and Takeaways from Chapter 2

- 98% of your thoughts today are identical to the ones you had yesterday and the day before.

- 80% of your thoughts are negative and 60% of those are negative thoughts about yourself.

- Instead of drawing conclusions, forming opinions, or, worst of all, making judgments, ASK QUESTIONS.

- The question is, **"What if _____ ?"** *(fill in the blank),* and follow that up with, **"What would that look like?"**

- You only have to *ask* the question. Answers will arrive all on their own.

- Asking questions engages our imaginations in a constructive way.

- You were created perfectly by a loving God, and, *"God doesn't make junk."*

- *"8 Master Keys that Unlock Your Total Health"* are ...
  - What you EAT
  - What you DRINK
  - What and How you BREATHE
  - How you EXERCISE (or don't!)
  - How you REST
  - What you THINK, FEEL, and BELIEVE
  - What you SPEAK
  - How you NURTURE YOUR SPIRIT

- The better choices you make, the easier it is for your original blueprint to express itself.

Chapter 3

How's Your Vibration?

Are you happy about your life today, who you are, where you work, whom you're with, and where you live?

In other words, is your life a source of joy to you and does it inspire a feeling of gratitude?

To the degree you can answer YES to these questions, your body's cells are vibrating at a high frequency. The odds of having physical illness, or even susceptibility to it, are very small indeed.

You probably wake up rested, with plenty of energy to go through your day feeling great. You're fun to be around. You work hard, but you balance your work and play, and just as importantly, you love someone and you *feel* loved.

Some people call this happiness. Others may call it impossible. Whatever you call it, it's all about energy. Your body is an electrochemical system; the energy that runs your body and the energy you generate is electrical. The source of this energy comes from chemical reactions that occur in liquid, mainly water.

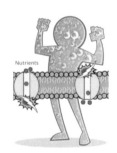

Because your body is electrical, it generates an electromagnetic field, or energy field, and radiates this field around itself. Scientists have long studied the human energy field, measured it, and categorized its characteristics, frequencies, and patterns. Dr. Valerie

Hunt invested most of her career measuring the human energy field. She identified certain frequencies and fluctuations with specific emotions and states of vitality.

What does all this mean to you?

Every cell in your body vibrates at certain frequencies. Frequencies and vibrations are measures of energy. When sperm meets egg, a new cell is formed. This new cell vibrates and every multiplication vibrates also at the same frequency. Nine months later, a complete human being is formed containing trillions of cells, all of which, in a healthy baby, are vibrating in harmony with one another.

- In a well-known experiment, individual living heart cells were placed in a Petri dish. At first, the cells vibrated at random frequencies, but very quickly, their vibrations organized into a single pulse.

- Swinging pendulums of clocks in a shop are known to become synchronized without any human intervention.

- Groups of women in close quarters for months or longer, begin to experience their monthly cycles at relatively the same time.

> **Your physical body, including your brain chemistry, responds to what you think, feel, and believe, just as much as it responds to your choices in any of the other *"Eight Master Keys."***

Foods also vibrate at various frequencies. For example, cooked meat and even well-cooked vegetables vibrate at a low frequency. They're

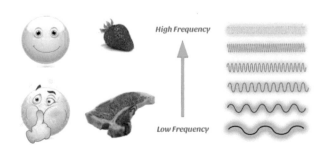

dead for the most part. Living foods, such as veggies you'd find in a fresh salad, vibrate at relatively high frequencies. The more alive your food, the more alive you are, because your body will adjust its overall vibration to match what you take in.

This same principle applies to what you see, hear, smell, taste, and touch:

- The sound of heavy metal music versus a soft lullaby
- The smell of dead fish versus that of a freshly cut ripe orange
- The taste of bitter versus sweet
- The touch of sandpaper versus velvet

The principle also applies to your emotions ... what you *FEEL.* Simply put, positive emotions have higher vibrational frequencies than

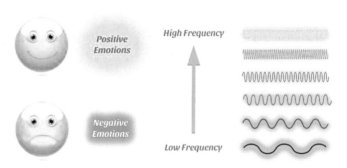

negative feelings. Therefore, the more intensely positive the emotion, the higher its frequency and the better you feel.

You can get some idea of how this works by responding in one of the following ways to the question, *"How are you?"* Try it and see what difference it makes in how you feel:

- "I feel good."
- "I feel terrible."
- "I feel excellent."

In the chapters that follow, we'll explore how your feelings can affect your physical health. We'll also discover how a genuine feeling of gratitude can become perhaps the most powerful and perpetually healing emotion of all.

> *Your immune system adjusts its actions*
> *to accommodate your vibrations.*

The genesis of "autoimmune" conditions

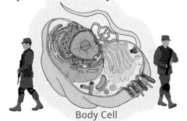

Proper Immune System Function

Body Cell

Your immune system is *designed* to keep your insides protected from a universe of germs, and it performs that job flawlessly ... unless you introduce feelings of frustration, dissatisfaction, or impatience at a high enough intensity, or over a long enough time – never mind more intense emotions, such as resentment, hatred, bitterness, or rage.

When these kinds of negative feelings swirl inside you, your cells vibrate at a lower frequency and your immune system begins to perceive them as the enemy from which it must protect *you*, and it begins to attack your own tissues and organs as if they were infected by an outside invader.

We call this phenomenon "auto-immune," and we give it fancy medical names like Lupus, Epstein-Barr, Fibromyalgia, chronic fatigue, rheumatoid arthritis, and lots of other commonly diagnosed conditions.

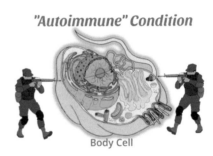

"Autoimmune" Condition

Body Cell

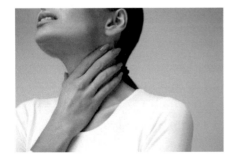

I worked with a young woman, early in my practice, whose immune system was completely overwhelmed by what to her was a life-threatening experience. She arrived home with a sore throat after a day at the beach with friends. She developed a high fever and even began hemorrhaging in her joints within a few days.

Doctors in at least three hospitals failed to find a cause, until her spinal fluid was tested and the bacteria was found that supposedly causes the disease known as bacterial meningitis.

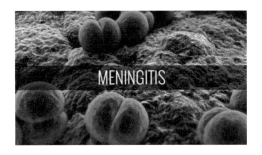

Meningitis is believed to be caused by an infection, so the young woman was isolated and treated with high-powered intravenous antibiotics, which could only be administered for a maximum of five days before they would wipe out her entire immune system. Her friends also had to be tested, due to the supposedly contagious nature of the disease, but none of them had any signs of infection.

Three days later, the young woman had not responded to the powerful antibiotics. Her parents were desperate, because the doctors had no plan B.

When the young woman's mother told me that her daughter's first symptom was a sore throat, I knew what had happened. I said, *"Your daughter's throat became sore because she wanted to scream or say something and she couldn't. Her body went into full blown emergency mode, which overwhelmed her immune system and allowed the bacteria to grow like a dandelion in May!"*

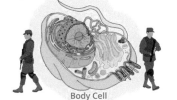

Proper Immune System Function

Body Cell

Once we identified the emotions during the event that happened several days earlier, and went through the steps of the *Heart, Soul and Spirit Cleanse*, the young woman's immune system got the message that the emergency was over and went back to its original job of keeping the bacteria in check. The same bacteria are in your spinal fluid right now, but your immune system keeps it under control.

When we finished the same *Heart, Soul and Spirit Cleanse* that you'll learn in a future chapter, the young woman could lift and move her head without pain within 10 minutes. She was up and walking the next day, and she left the hospital three days later with no ill effects.

The fact is, we build whole belief systems around diseases and their imagined causes. We can observe the chemical markers in blood work and see physical changes under a microscope. Most often, the blame is put on genetics, family history, latent viruses, and infection.

Even systemic inflammation can be caused as much by negative emotions as by poor diet; but whenever we get in trouble health-wise, standard treatment protocols focus only on trying to relieve symptoms or stopping the physical changes in cells and tissues. The truth is, no outside measures you take address the real cause, because your emotional responses to situations, circumstances, or relationships are not directly observable with standard lab tests or by physical examination.

Medicine treats the conditions it can name with medications. Even if a so-called chemical imbalance is detected in someone diagnosed as bipolar, for example, the only medical option is psychiatry. No matter which way you turn, you're going to be taking one or more drugs – and all drugs do is treat, or mask, symptoms.

> *"You can never treat enough symptoms to get to the cause."*
> Dr. M.T. Morter, Jr.

 ## Nutshells and Takeaways from Chapter 3

- Your body is an electrochemical energy system that generates and radiates an electromagnetic field.

- Every cell in your body vibrates at a certain frequency. Food choices, along with thoughts and feelings either increase or decrease your vibrations.

- The more positive your emotions, the higher your vibration and the better you feel.

- Your immune system adjusts its actions to accommodate your vibrations.

- Autoimmune conditions are the result of negative emotions felt over a long enough period of time or at a high enough intensity to make your immune system think that your own body is a "germ" that needs to be eliminated.

- We build whole belief systems around diseases and their imagined causes.

- Standard treatment protocols focus only on trying to relieve symptoms.

- You can never treat enough symptoms to get to the cause.

You are not an accident of creation and your life isn't a series of lucky steps, terrible mistakes, and near misses.

Your Creator knew exactly where you'd be today and all the steps it would take to bring you to this page now.

Chapter 4

The Spirit-Mind-Body Connection

The relatively new science of epigenetics demonstrates that no matter who you are, where you're from, or the condition you're in, your state of health and well-being is more directly tied to your spiritual, mental, and emotional states, than your family history or genetics.

The truth is that your ability to heal physically, mentally, and emotionally, is intimately woven together with your thoughts, feelings and beliefs about yourself, the situations, circumstances and relationships throughout your life, and even your relationship to God.

> **How you think, feel, and believe is virtually set by the time you're seven years-old.**

I once worked with a young man who had been diagnosed as bipolar on the basis of his behavior and family history. At home around his wife and kids, he demonstrated classic signs of a bipolar personality, and his mother had been a raging bipolar woman, who was hospitalized several times when he was a young boy.

As logical as his diagnosis seemed, I couldn't find any evidence of it. I told him and his wife that I didn't think he was bipolar at all; instead, he'd been playing out exactly the behavior that had been modeled in front of him from the time he was a baby. He believed his mother's erratic behavior to be normal and even worthy of duplicating. When he became a dad, however, the behavior he grew up observing in someone he loved, and knowing no alternative, threatened to break up his family.

By the time the young man was old enough to think for himself, the patterns of his own behavior had already been set. The remarkable part of his story was that, unlike his mother, he had avoided hospitalization.

He was completely free of his mother's influence in less than 3 months of beginning our work together, and he became the husband that his wife had fallen in love with and the dad that his children adored.

What's "magic" about seven years old?

Before you reach seven years old, you believe *everything* you're told and you assume that the behaviors you observe around you most of the time are *normal*. You discover what is and is not acceptable by observing the consequences of others' behavior, or even more profoundly, by *experiencing* the consequences of your own behavior.

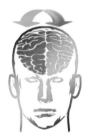

By seven years old, structures and connections within your brain have developed to allow your right and left brain hemispheres to communicate, which is when critical thinking and reasoning begin. Until then, you simply absorb and believe what others teach you about yourself and your world, either by verbal repetition or by example.

Since virtually everything you understand and believe by age seven has been determined by others, much of your own self-image, thought patterns, perspectives, and beliefs, are limited by their examples.

> You develop "belief habits" as surely as you develop nutritional habits. Your quality of life in every area is determined in large part by what you think about, what you really believe, and how you feel about both.

The so-called "mind-body connection" is much more profound than that term suggests, which is why Barbara Brown and I refer to it in our books as the *spirit-mind-body connection.* The *"iron rule"* of cancer is one of the most startling applications of this concept.

German physician, Ryke Geerd Hamer, developed the *iron rule* of cancer following an exhaustive study after he developed testicular cancer. Dr. Hamer's son was shot while on holiday in the Mediterranean and died 3 months later. Dr. Hamer's cancer was diagnosed soon after his son's death.

In over 20,000 cancer cases, Dr. Hamer found that he could trace, without exception, the development of each person's cancer to a severe emotional shock for which they were completely unprepared. He found, through brain scan imaging, that the shock left a "dark shadow" on the brain in the exact location of the body structure that developed the cancer.

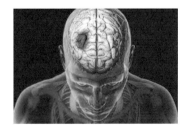

Dr. Hamer's *iron rule* has never been disproven since he presented his findings at a medical conference in Vienna, in 1978, but few physicians know about it and, as a result, neither do their patients.

Here's a quick summary of the *iron rule:*

1. Every cancer starts with a brutal "psychic trauma" – a highly traumatic emotional shock – experienced by the person in a sense of profound loneliness, as the most serious event that the person has ever known.

2. The way the person "colors" the experience; that is, the *emotions* they feel and the *pictures* they paint of the experience, determines what area of the brain suffers a breakdown, which Dr. Hamer was able to demonstrate on MRI studies.

3. The area of breakdown in the brain determines where tumor cells develop in the body.

4. Dr. Hamer concluded that what medicine calls metastasis is actually new primary tumors brought about by new insults. Even a cancer diagnosis, he found, can cause further trauma and additional areas of "breakdown."

5. The good news in Dr. Hamer's conclusions was that when the original insult or conflict was resolved inside a person (i.e., the person changed how he or she *felt* about the experience), the "damaged" area in the brain began to wall itself off as part of a healing process. This shut off the signals to the tumors, which stopped growing or disappeared entirely.

Dr. Hamer's findings were corroborated independently by Dr. Brendan O'Reagan, in his 1993 study of what's known as *"spontaneous remission"* in 10,000 cancer cases. Spontaneous remission means that the disease process has suddenly stopped for no apparent reason.

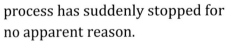

Barbara's perspective from her years in ministry is that cancer results from a *"death wish."* People who perceive themselves to be trapped in dark and desperate situations or hopeless relationships, from which they see no escape, may declare – sometimes out loud – *"I just want to die."* If this desire is strong enough and is repeated long enough, the body will respond as it does in Dr. Hamer's scenario of a "brutal psychic trauma." This one, however, is self-inflicted, as if the body says, *"Got it. I'll help you."*

A close relative, after decades as a single woman, married a man whom she had known for many years. The whole relationship seemed to be perfectly orchestrated and the couple appeared to be a perfect fit for one another. Within about two years, her husband's personality showed its true colors and he became verbally abusive. Divorce was unthinkable and my relative felt helpless to change the situation.

Within a few months, she began to show signs of serious mental illness. She became delusional and was in danger of having to be hospitalized or committed to an institution.

When I learned how serious her condition was, I insisted that she fly out immediately to stay with my family. In less than 24 hours after her arrival, she was perfectly relaxed and normal.

Although the example above didn't result in cancer, it demonstrates what may sound like a frightening principle:

> **Your mind can take your body out of a situation or relationship that you want to escape badly enough by whatever means it can.**

My relative was days away from becoming a drugged out psychiatric patient. She would also have succeeded in freeing herself from a marriage she could no longer bear. Mission accomplished.

Time after time in practice, I found that the *iron rule* applied to nearly *every* condition, not just cancer. I noticed that a kind of "short circuiting" in the autonomic part of a person's nervous system was at the root of his or her pain, illness or dysfunction. Actual healing only began, and proceeded unhindered and unhampered, when we corrected what science calls

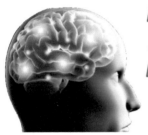

"negative memory engrams" – patterns of thoughts, feelings and beliefs – that were incongruent or out of sync with present time, or ran contrary to the person's sense of inherent worth and divine design. We'll examine this process in the next chapter.

A sign on the reception counter of our office in New Hampshire read, *"God Bless You."* One woman came in, pointed to the sign and told Barbara, *"I am God."* When Barbara told me about the woman's remark later, I said, *"Well, she's not doing a very good job if she's coming to see me."*

It has been our experience that the greater your *faith* in God, the greater your potential for healing, and the less you interfere with its process. Call it *"faith-healing"* if you like. After all, the greatest healer of all said, **"Your faith has healed you"** (Matthew 9:22, NIV).

> **What if all healing is ultimately faith-healing?**
> **What would that look like?**

As another wise man once said, **"For as a man thinks within himself so he is,"** or, **"as a woman thinks within herself so she is"** (Proverbs 23:7, NASB).

Barbara's story of her miraculous healing from muscular dystrophy (in Chapter 1) is a great illustration of how the *spirit-mind-body connection* works at its best.

The next time you get into trouble physically, mentally, or emotionally, think about what you were thinking *before* the trouble started. More often than not, you'll find your answer.

In the next chapter, we'll look at how to change your thoughts, feelings and beliefs to let go of the past, forgive every experience, learn from it, and thereby heal your mind, memory and emotions.

 Nutshells and Takeaways from Chapter 4

- The science of epigenetics demonstrates that your state of health and well-being is more directly tied to your spiritual, mental, and emotional states, than your family history or genetics.

- Your ability to heal is intimately woven together with your thoughts, feelings and beliefs about yourself, the situations, circumstances and relationships throughout your life, and even your relationship to God.

- How you think, feel, and believe is virtually set by the time you're seven years-old.

- Before you reach seven years-old, you believe *everything* you're told about yourself and your world, either by verbal repetition or by example.

- You develop "belief habits" as surely as you develop nutritional habits.

- The *"iron rule"* of cancer is an example of the *spirit-mind-body connection.*

- The *iron rule* states that ...

1. Every cancer starts with a brutal "psychic trauma" – a highly traumatic emotional shock – experienced in a sense of loneliness, and perceived as the most serious the person has ever known.

2. The way the person sees and feels about the experience determines what area of the brain suffers a breakdown.

3. The area of breakdown in the brain determines where tumor cells develop.

4. Metastasis is actually new primary tumors and even a cancer diagnosis can cause additional areas of "breakdown."

5. When the person resolved their feelings about the experience, the healing process began. Tumors stopped growing and sometimes disappeared entirely.

- Cancer may result from a "death wish," when someone feels trapped in a hopeless situation or relationship, and thinks, *"I just want to die."*

- Your body will take you out of a situation or relationship by whatever means it can if you want it badly enough.

- The *iron rule* applies to nearly *every* condition.

- *"Negative memory engrams"* are patterns of thoughts, feelings and beliefs that are out of sync with present time, or run contrary to your sense of inherent worth and divine design.

- The greater your *faith* in God, the greater your potential for healing, and the less you interfere with its process.

- Jesus said, **"Your faith has healed you"** (Matthew 9:22, NIV).

- What if all healing is ultimately faith-healing?

- King Solomon said, **_"For as a man thinks within himself so he is,"_** or, **_"as a woman thinks within herself so she is"_** (Proverbs 23:7, NASB).

- Barbara's story of miraculous healing from muscular dystrophy (Chapter 1) illustrates how the _spirit-mind-body connection_ works at its best.

- The next time you get into trouble, physically, mentally, or emotionally, think about what you were thinking _before_ the trouble started. More often than not, you'll find your answer.

You are free to make your choices.
You are not free from the consequences of those choices.

Chapter 5

How to Change Your Thoughts, Feelings, and Beliefs to Heal Your Body, Mind, and Spirit

Barbara Brown and I refer to the *spirit-mind-body connection*, because healing involves all three and in that order, as a kind of *"chain of command."*

Your spirit is what makes you alive. Without your spirit, your mind and body don't function at all. Ideally, your mind gets its marching orders from your spirit, and your brain transfers the instructions to your body. Your mind is certainly capable of running off on its own – which we all know only too well – but it can't function at all without the life of your spirit.

Your body simply responds to instructions from your conscious and subconscious mind. Your body carries out those instructions and the result is how you feel physically. Even though you pay most attention to how you feel physically, your body is last in line and, unless you just stepped on a nail, the problem is located higher up the *chain of command* in your mind or spirit.

If you leave one element out of the *spirit-mind-body* system, or change the order, the process we're about to go

through doesn't work.

You may be surprised to discover that science and Scripture actually *agree* with and support one another.

- Principles contained in both science and Scripture operate all the time, whether you believe them or not.

- Scriptural principles and scientific laws are practical, applicable, and reliable, whether you believe them or not.

- Merging science and Scripture becomes *essential* to gain a clear understanding of how your body works, how you get sick, how you get healthy, and how you stay that way.

 Cellular biologist, Bruce Lipton, in his book, *The Biology of Belief*, explodes the *"central dogma"* of medical science – the myth, really – that genetics determines health and disease. He explains and demon-strates clearly how DNA expression can be determined or altered by *feelings and beliefs*!

The following are principles from science and Scripture that operate all the time, no matter who you are or where you're from; what your gender, race, or ethnicity is; or what your beliefs may be.

- One of the greatest realizations you can have is that you are a *spiritual* being undergoing a *physical* experience, not the other way around. When you live like a *physical* being *looking* for a spiritual experience, you are 180 degrees out of phase with how God created you.

- Pain, illness, disease, or dysfunction becomes the inevitable result of being out of alignment with God's original blueprint. Likewise, healing is just as inevitable and unstoppable when we align and agree with God's original design.

- Your body is a stimulus-response organism. Of course, there's a lot of complexity within that cycle, but that's the simplest explanation of how your body works.

Stimulus (HEAT)

Response (LET GO)

- Your body is also designed to be self-organizing, self-healing, and self-regulating. Your body doesn't think, judge or reason; rather, it responds to external and internal stimuli for the sole purpose of survival.

Stimulus (HEAT)

Response (LET GO)

Survive!

- The responses your body makes are *perfect* for the stimuli that make them necessary. Those responses don't always *feel* good (we call those symptoms), but they are perfect nevertheless.

Stimulus **Response**

PERFECT!

- Your body is constantly cleansing, rebuilding and supporting the life within every cell and between all cells. Your body does the best it can with the nutritional, emotional, and spiritual environment *you* provide.

- Your body responds according to its *design*, not your *desire*. This explains why vibrant health seems to *evade* some people who genuinely *want* to be well.

- Your body runs mostly on a kind of "autopilot." When you get on an airplane, you may think that the pilot and co-pilot are steering the plane toward its destination. Most of your flight, however, is actually accomplished by the "autopilot" system. In fact, some planes even land on autopilot.

Try counting your heart beats and your breathing rate at the same time for at least a minute; it's almost impossible, even for a few seconds. Now imagine having to control these two vital functions, while adjusting your hormone levels, body temperature, digestive juices, and kidney filtration every day ... and do it while you sleep!

Thank God for your body's autopilot!

- Your "autonomic" nervous system controls almost every function in your body. It responds to outside stimuli coming through your senses, and internal stimuli coming from its own monitoring system. Your sensory nerves carry more than 10,000 impulses per second to an area of your brain, called the Reticular Activating System (RAS), which acts like the most sophisticated data processing computer you can imagine.

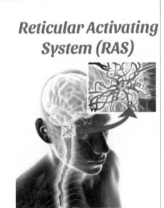

- More than 99 percent of all the information coming into the RAS is *discarded* as *unimportant!* Only the sensory information "judged" by your RAS as important for your immediate survival is passed along. This means that less than 1 percent of all impulses bombarding your brain-stem every second – are considered worthy of a response!

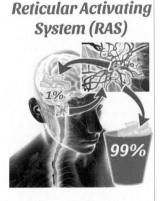

What an awesome autopilot!

We'll go through several steps to help you change your thoughts, feelings and beliefs to heal your body, mind, and spirit in the next chapters.

First, we thought you might enjoy learning a shortcut.

When we were kids, we loved finding shortcuts from place to place, and when we couldn't find one, we made our own, through fields and over fences. There's something truly rewarding about finding a faster way to a destination, or a shorter process that achieves the same goal as everyone else, *only sooner.*

The world's best shortcut to healing your spirit, mind, and body, is a simple instruction from one of the greatest teachers to walk the Earth:

> In his first letter to the Thessalonians, the Apostle Paul wrote, *"In everything be giving thanks, for this is the will of God in Christ Jesus for you."*
> (1 Thessalonians 5:18, CLNT)

"In everything …" Everything means exactly *that*: the good, the bad and the ugly; not just the situations and relationships we like, but those we don't. Not just the parts of our lives that we're happy with, but the parts we wish were different. Not just the memories we enjoy, but the ones we wish we could forget. Not just the experiences we're already grateful for, but the ones we wish hadn't happened at all.

"In everything be giving thanks …" Genuine, heartfelt gratitude is one of the highest frequencies on the emotional "scale." It's even stronger than love, in our experience, because it *includes* love. Giving thanks has the power to

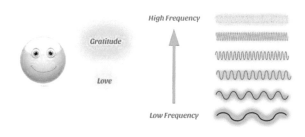

strengthen you in ways that are hard to describe, but you know them when you feel them. Giving thanks has the power to virtually dissolve anything negative, including illness.

> **"The feeling is the fuel behind the healing."**
> (Stewart Grayson, First Church of Religious Science)

"In everything be giving thanks, for this is the will of God for you." If you ever wondered what the will of God is for you, here it is in plain language. When you *are* giving thanks, you're *fulfilling* the will of God, pure and simple. What the apostle Paul *doesn't* say is that when you *aren't* giving thanks, you aren't fulfilling the will of God!

> "Gratitude can transform common days into thanksgivings, turn routine jobs into joy, and change ordinary opportunities into blessings."
>
> - William Arthur Ward

Look at the instruction one more time: **"In everything be giving thanks, for this is the will of God in Christ Jesus for you."**

The underpinning for this principle to work is **"in Christ Jesus."** The meaning is actually, *"inside Christ Jesus."* It's a location, and an inescapable part of how to sustain real gratitude, especially for the circumstances in your life that you would have left out if you had been the architect.

Think about the example from our last chapter of the young man whose mother had been bipolar throughout his most formative years. He can't pretend that she was like other moms, or that his upbringing had been some other way. His healing was complete when his gratitude for what he learned throughout his traumatic childhood was greater than the wounds of his mother's personality.

Here he was, loved completely by his wife, and adored by two little daughters, who were the most precious jewels in his life. He wouldn't trade them for anything, so he found genuine gratitude in his heart for his life today, which made all the steps worthwhile that led him here. His gratitude included growing up with a bipolar mother and thinking that was normal!

When the man set his gratitude in the firm foundation, *"inside Christ Jesus,"* he experienced a certainty that was unquestionable and permanently sustaining. He began to view his early life as essential for his current life even to be possible, let alone succeed. His memories became assets rich with valuable lessons, rather than liabilities full of  hurt and remorse. He could see that his upbringing was part of God's loving purpose, rather than the Creator's divine neglect or punishment; it was all part of God's perfect design, not some tragic accident.

 **"In Christ Jesus"** conveys a location where we can see that God's purpose and love permeate every situation, circumstance and relationship throughout our lives. Christ Himself was faced with far greater challenges than we are, but He knew that the purpose for His life was worth the cost. Most importantly, He knew that God loved Him and wouldn't leave Him dead.

What if you had the same realization? What if you discovered what my formerly bipolar patient did and that Christ Himself knew? What if you knew that every part of your life has been entirely purposed and engineered by a God Who loves you and won't leave you dead either?

Then, even though you may not *grasp* the purpose, or *like* everything about how it operates, you can, **"In everything be giving thanks, for this is the will of God in Christ Jesus for you."**

Barbara Brown and I have observed over and over that when you align yourself with God's design – spiritually, mentally, and physically – health, happiness and success are the inevitable outcomes. Just like my formerly bipolar patient's experience, in this location, illness can't hold you hostage.

We could summarize the shortcut to the *Heart, Soul and Spirit Cleanse* in a single sentence:

> *"You're either gonna get grateful or you're gonna get sick."*
> Even shorter: *"Get grateful or get sick."*

Not the most formal English, granted, but it makes the point.

When a patient came in one day declaring, *"I figured it out! I know what the problem is!"*

"Great," I said, *"What is it?"* She had made progress up to that point, but hadn't had the kind of breakthrough that we expect.

"It's my job!" She said with great certainty.

"That's great," I said, *"so when will you be changing your job?"*

"Oh," she said, *"I can't change my job; I need my job."*

"So, what are you going to do?" I asked.

"I don't know," she said, *"but I know that my job is the problem."*

"Well, you only have one other choice," I said, *"change the way you perceive your job and the people there. Give thanks for every part of your job – especially the parts you don't like – that you are excited to get there in the morning, and satisfied when you leave at the end of the day."*

She was thoughtful for a moment and then said, *"So ... how I perceive my job and how I feel about the people is the real problem?"*

"You got it," I said.

When you are unhappy in any circumstance or relationship, all you can do is change your location, or change how you *see* your location; how you *perceive* it or *feel* about it. Of course, if you change your location, the people and surroundings may be different, but *you* are the same, and you'll soon discover that you brought your "stuff" with you.

As Barbara says, *"Whether you're running to or from something, you take the same dirt with you."*

One of Barbara's great life-principles is this:

"God took you a way you wouldn't have gone to teach you what you needed to learn."

When you have learned what you need to learn, then you'll be free to go or stay, because you won't be running to, or away from, anything.

When you're free to stay, you're free to go.
When you're free to go, you're free to stay.

In the next chapter, we'll explore the first four steps of the *Heart, Soul and Spirit Cleanse*. You'll also find this cleanse outlined in the book, *Your Personal Roadmap to Whole Body Cleansing*. A condensed version also appears in the book, *The Magic of pH*.

Nutshells and Takeaways from Chapter 5

- Healing involves the spirit, mind, and body, in that order, like a *"chain of command."*

  - Your spirit is what makes you alive.
  - Your mind gets its marching orders from your spirit.
  - Your brain transfers the instructions to your body.
  - Your body carries out the instructions it receives from your brain.
  - The result is how you feel.

- Principles contained in both science and Scripture operate all the time, whether you believe them or not.

- Merging science and Scripture is *essential* to understand how your body works.

- The *"central dogma"* of medical science is the myth that genetics determines health and disease.

- DNA expression responds to *feelings and beliefs.*

- You are a *spiritual* being undergoing a *physical* experience, not the other way around.

- Pain, illness, disease, or dysfunction is the result of being out of alignment with God's original blueprint.

- Healing is inevitable and unstoppable when you align and agree with God's original design.

- Your body is a stimulus-response organism.

- Your body is self-organizing, self-healing, and self-regulating.

- Your body doesn't think, judge or reason; it responds to external and internal stimuli for the sole purpose of survival.

- Your body's responses are *perfect* for the stimuli that make them necessary.

- Symptoms are your body's responses that don't feel good, but they're still perfect.

- Your body does the best it can to survive the nutritional, emotional, and spiritual environment *you* provide.

- Your body responds according to its *design*, not your *desire*.

- Your body runs mostly on "autopilot."

- More than 10,000 impulses per second bombard your brainstem, your senses, and your internal monitoring system.

- More than 99 percent of all incoming information is *discarded* as *unimportant!*

- Less than 1 percent of all incoming information is even considered worthy of a response!

- The best shortcut to healing your spirit, mind, and body, is, **"In everything be giving thanks, for this is the will of God in Christ Jesus for you"** (1 Thessalonians 5:18, CLNT).

- Gratitude is one of the highest frequencies on the emotional "scale," even stronger than love.

- Giving thanks has the power to virtually dissolve anything negative, including illness.

- *"The feeling is the fuel behind the healing"* (Stewart Grayson, First Church of Religious Science).

- **"In Christ Jesus"** conveys a location where we can see that God's purpose and love permeate every situation, circumstance and relationship throughout our lives.

- What if you knew that the God Who loves you won't leave you dead, just like He didn't leave Jesus dead?

- The quickest shortcut through the *Heart, Soul and Spirit Cleanse* is, *"You're either gonna get grateful or you're gonna get sick."* Even shorter: *"Get grateful or get sick."*

- When you are unhappy in any circumstance or relationship, you have only two choices: Change your location, or change how you *see* your location; how you *perceive* it or feel *about* it.

- *"If you're running to or from something, you take the same dirt with you."*
  (Barbara Brown, MSE)

- When you're free to stay, you're free to go. When you're free to go, you're free to stay.

- *"God took you a way you wouldn't have gone to teach you what you needed to learn."*
  (Barbara Brown, MSE)

Take advantage of the online resources for this book at ItsOK.WholeLifeWholeHealth.com

Chapter 6

Make Friends with Your Symptoms

The order in which injury, illness *and* healing seem to progress is as follows:

- First in your **Spirit** – through your emotions;
- Second, in your **Soul** (Mind) – through your beliefs and memories;
- Third, in your **Body** – through what we call symptoms.

Science has no real understanding of the spirit, much less any explanation of its substance, nature, or action. It's clear, however, that your spirit is your *life*, or life essence, if you like. No matter how you view spirit, there is no life without it. The Scriptures use breath to illustrate spirit, which imparts life to the "soul." Your soul is the seat of your awareness, which ceases upon death.

> *"And the Lord God formed man of the dust of the ground, and breathed into his nostrils the breath of life; and man became a living soul."* (Genesis 2:7, King James Version)

We humans focus mainly on our bodies and we become experts on what hurts and where; but our bodies are last in line and they're only along for the ride that started in our spirits.

We all *think* we know what symptoms are, but let's define the term here, because it will help us as we go through the process that follows:

Symptoms are simply responses that you can feel in your body, which result from *"timing problems"* due to trauma, toxicity, and your own thoughts, emotions and beliefs.

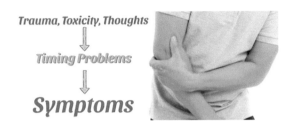

Trauma, Toxicity, Thoughts
⇓
Timing Problems
⇓
Symptoms

What is a "timing problem"?

A timing problem is any function in the body that occurs when it shouldn't, or doesn't occur when it should. One of the best examples of a timing problem is so-called "acid reflux," or GERD. Mental and emotional stress tends to shut down digestion, stopping stomach acid production when food is present. As food sits in the stomach undigested, it ferments and bubbles up into the esophagus. With no mucus-producing cells to protect its delicate lining, as are found in the stomach, classic "heartburn" or reflux symptoms occur when acid in the fermentation process bubbles up into the esophagus.

On the other side of the timing problem, the stomach may produce acid when no food is present. In this case, stomach acid can eat away at the stomach lining over time and lead to an ulcer.

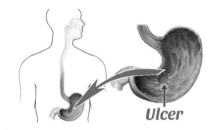

Ulcer

People with reflux symptoms, or a diagnosis of GERD (Gastro-Esophageal Reflux Disease) generally have a *deficiency* of stomach acid, not an overabundance. GERD patients may also have bacteria present in their stomachs, called Helicobacter pylori (H. pylori).

Proper Immune System Function

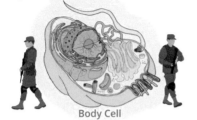

Body Cell

Medical treatment is, of course, antibiotics; however, just like the bacteria that "causes" meningitis, H. pylori is always present, but is an opportunistic organism. Like other bacteria, it can only flourish in the right environment and is normally kept in check by a robust immune system.

Remedies for "heartburn" began with baking soda or bismuth, and progressed to "Alka-

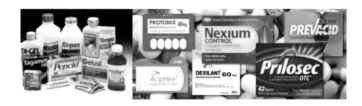

Seltzer" and progressively stronger "antacids." Today's more "sophisticated" medications for reflux or GERD effectively shut off the brain's messages to the stomach. This stops acid production, but the person can't digest protein, a process that occurs almost exclusively in the stomach!

Wouldn't you think that someone along the way would have stopped long enough to ask, *"Why do we keep needing stronger drugs? Is it possible that the real cause lies somewhere else?"* By the time you've finished reading this book, you'll know enough to ask that kind of question for yourself at the first sign of a symptom!

The overgrowth of opportunistic organisms, such as viruses, bacteria, fungus and yeast, is itself evidence of a timing problem. When your habits enable the proper environment inside your body to dominate, unfriendly organisms cannot gain a foothold and proliferate. The diseases that these organisms are associated with, therefore, cannot occur.

Louis Pasteur's greatest rival was renowned scientist, Antoine Béchamp. Pasteur is best known for his *"germ theory of disease,"* which states simply that microbes cause disease by invading the body from the outside. Béchamp proposed exactly the opposite in his *"Host [or Cellular] Theory."* He

Pasteur vs. Béchamp

stated that microorganisms (bacteria, yeast, or fungus, for example) are particles that already exist in all living organisms. These microorganisms multiply in a friendly environment – its "terrain" or "soil" – and can even mutate to accommodate changes in the body's "terrain" or "soil."

Although western medicine is still "all in" with Pasteur's theory, there is ample scientific evidence and clinical experience to support this principle:

Germs don't cause disease; they are opportunists. The germ is nothing; the terrain is everything.

You provide an environment inside your body that is either favorable or unfavorable for microorganisms to grow and proliferate. You create the environment by the choices you make every day in the areas of the "8 Master Keys" that we discussed in Chapter 2.

8 Master Keys
That Unlock Your Total Health

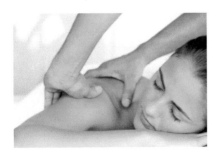

Pleasant versus Unpleasant Symptoms

Pleasant symptoms are part of experiences we enjoy, but we pay almost no attention to how good we feel, as opposed to the attention we pay to pain or illness. I used to tell patients that they may not leap out of the office, shrieking, *"'Eureka, I'm healed!' Instead, you'll realize one day, 'Hey! That thing that was bugging me is gone!'"*

Normal doesn't feel like anything, so it doesn't get our attention. On the other hand, pain is something that we'll do almost anything to avoid or get rid of as fast as possible.

NORMAL
doesn't feel like anything

PAIN
gets our attention!

Unpleasant, undesired symptoms that we readily focus on, accompany experiences we wish were different, but which we are unable to change at the time they occur. The memories of these experiences can cause serious trouble to our health sooner or later.

Here is an example of how this works:

A young woman who suffered from debilitating seizures for 18 months had been forced to quit her job and move back into her parents' home. No one had found a cause, and no medication had succeeded in controlling the seizures. The young woman's mother had to drive her to the appointment, because her driver's license had been disallowed by one of the neurologists she had seen. The young woman was understandably despondent.

A simple saliva pH test indicated that the young woman was in full-blown emergency mode, but her healing mode was still functioning. Her experience during a dental appointment, where seizures began, turned out to be only a secondary insult, even though as soon as the dentist inserted a needle containing Novocaine, she had the first seizure.

The primary insult came a week earlier, also during a dental appointment, when she was unable to get the dentist's or the assistant's attention while they worked on  her mouth, which was blocked open. The doctor and her assistant were discussing their weekend plans, oblivious to the young woman's discomfort. She left that appointment angry and still in pain. At another dentist's office a week later, her nervous system, already in a state of heightened emergency, simply could not accommodate one more stimulus in a similar environment. The energy that had been built up discharged all at once.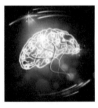

The diagnosis was a seizure condition, but the stimulus was the suppressed emotions that could not find an outlet during the first dental appointment. The sense of disrespect and carelessness shown by two health care professionals kept the "coals burning" until the split-second pain of the Novocaine needle at the second dental appointment was felt. Seizures continued intermittently after the second insult, because the original stimulus continued to sound the alarm in the woman's subconscious.

When I described this scenario to the young lady at our first meeting, a look of recognition and profound relief came over her. She said to her mother, *"Haven't I been saying almost exactly the same thing from the beginning?"*

After a brief energy balancing procedure, her nervous system got the message that the emergency was over and the young woman's seizures stopped completely. Over the following days and weeks, the young woman's hope returned as her body resumed its normal function.

Why did the young woman's body continue to respond to her perception of an emergency in the dentist's office *AFTER* she left? Why did the young woman's immune system continue to be overwhelmed by an emergency that was over in less than 15 minutes?

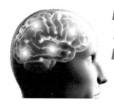

Negative Memory Engrams

Negative Memory Engrams

Pain, illness or dysfunction that continues after an emergency is over is affected by a neurological phenomenon called a *"negative memory engram."* The same is true when conditions linger after a *perceived* emergency (i.e., a "bear" you only *think* about chasing you) has been resolved.

Real vs. Imagined or Remembered

Engrams are literal neurological phenomena that occur in the brain. Engrams keep the memory of a trauma active in the subconscious, along with the body's survival responses, as if the event were still happening.

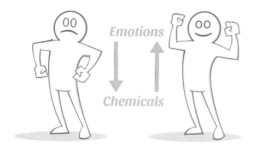

Positive emotions that we experience immediately *before* a traumatic event are "bushwhacked" *during* a trauma, and are "glued" to the negative memory engram. As a result, we tend to avoid feeling these positive emotions later on.

Here's how this phenomenon works:

A three year-old boy moved with his family into a brand new house. Mom and Dad showed him his room and gave him a coloring book and some crayons to play with, while they brought the family's belongings into their new home.

The little boy sat in the middle of his new room with his crayons and coloring book. He colored happily for a while in his big empty room,  until he looked up at the empty walls. He began to imagine coloring on the walls as if they were a gigantic coloring book. He felt inspired and creative. When he drew the first line with his dark blue crayon, he felt joyful, and as he drew more lines with more colors, he felt free and even satisfied...

 ...Then, Dad walked in the room. He shouted, *"No, No, No, No, No!"* The little boy was startled by the sound of Dad's voice. He had never heard that sound, or seen that look in Dad's eyes before.

Suddenly, a profound feeling of fear replaced the little boy's feelings of being inspired, creative, joyful, free, and satisfied. The physical pain that followed was recorded, along with the humiliation that the little boy felt in the aftermath of the immediate experience, as Mom came in to see what all the fuss was about.

From that day forward, the little boy felt afraid anytime he felt inspired, creative, joyful, free, or satisfied. He developed ways to avoid going too far into these emotions, because the negative memory engrams kept them in check as a survival mechanism.

Memory is permanent, and every experience is recorded and cataloged with a sort of time stamp and intensity rating. Healing only begins when a new message that the emergency is over reaches the same area of the  brain at the same intensity as the memory of the original insult. Until then, the body will continue in survival mode and healing is impossible.

The woman with meningitis from an earlier chapter and the one above with seizures are excellent examples of how negative memory engrams can affect health dramatically and frustrate almost any medical treatment. They are also testimonies to how quickly engrams can be effectively silenced and

how rapidly healing can progress. When new information – a new stimulus – reaches the same area of memory, with the same or higher level of intensity as the recorded trauma, healing begins immediately.

The laws of healing – as well as pain and disease – are universal. God has designed within you a miraculous and fool-proof process, which, when recognized, honored, and properly followed, enables healing to occur, often beyond our ability to comprehend, let alone explain it.

How all this works in four steps

STEP ONE: **Your "*Emergency*" mode is triggered by an "*alarm bell*" during an experience: a car accident, a dental appointment, or even a heated argument.**

We think of these alarms as "stress," but stress is simply any stimulus that requires your body to change. Stress is neither good nor bad; in fact, it's essential for survival. If it weren't for stress, you'd never get out of bed, and an apple would kill you, because your body wouldn't respond to the "stress" of an apple to digest it.

> Endocrinologist, Dr. Hans Selye, demonstrated that stress could cause diseases like heart attacks, strokes, kidney disease and rheumatoid arthritis.

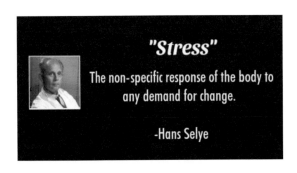

Even the *perception* of stress can trigger an alarm. Have you ever taken a walk in the woods and jumped suddenly, because you barely spotted a long dark "something" in your path. Your subconscious perceived a snake, when the object was only a stick. Perhaps an ancestor was bitten by a snake while walking in the woods and the engram was passed down through generations. Of course, this is only a theory, but it's as good as any, and it makes the point about survival taking priority over all else, including reason.

Almost any thought about finances, politics, or marital challenges, for example, can trigger an alarm. Barbara Brown and I call these stress-producing images in our minds, *"bears in the woods."* Bears are everywhere: spouse bears, work bears, kid bears, money bears; the woods are full of them and you can't find a gun big enough to shoot them all!

What if we changed how we felt about the bears in our lives? What would that look like? Dr. Selye suggested that, *"Adopting the right attitude can convert a negative stress into a positive one."*

The emergency, *"fight-or-flight"* response is inborn, automatic, and necessary for survival. We can even see it in the womb when a fetus jumps as it responds violently to a sudden, loud noise.

Outside the womb, alarms are triggered during events that we wish weren't happening. During the event, our neurological systems ring alarms that send every other system in our bodies – cardiovascular, hormonal, digestive, muscular, etc. – into emergency survival mode. Positive emotions we felt *before* an event happened are superseded by negative emotions that accompany and follow the event, which run in the background like a computer loop in subconscious memory for the rest of our lives.

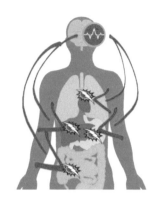

A friend of mine was driving through an intersection when a red car hit his car on the passenger's side. We worked through the effects of the accident, but he always approached that intersection with added caution from then on; and, if he ever saw a red car out of the corner of his eye, he would automatically brace himself as if expecting an impact.

It's easy to ignore or dismiss the first "alarm" consciously as simply another in a long line of changes you don't like. You'll hear people describe this phenomenon: *"I knew something wasn't right,"* they'll say, *"but I just couldn't put my finger on it,"* or, *"I thought it would go away,"* or, *"I just didn't think it was that big a deal."*

Your body's emergency survival system is supposed to kick in for *real* events that threaten your survival, like a bear coming out of the woods. Your pupils dilate for

maximum vision and blood flow increases to the lower limbs to run away as fast as you can. In some instances, blood may flow to the upper limbs to fight for survival. Emergencies shut off activity in some parts of our bodies too, like digestion, because you can't run from a bear and digest your lunch at the same time.

Your body is designed to handle short term, real threats to survival that should last only seconds; long enough to run or be eaten; long enough to fight or die trying.

Your body is not designed to tell the difference between real bears and the ones you think about. It responds exactly the same way, and when emergencies continue over hours,

days, months or even years, systems in your body become exhausted, one by one, until symptoms show up that compel you to seek help.

A patient who came in after a car accident made rapid progress over a period of weeks, but then, her progress simply stopped and her last remaining symptom, a pain in her left hip, would not resolve.

Finally, I asked if she had anything to eat or drink in the car when the accident happened. My question was to determine what senses were involved *during* the trauma. I had already asked if she had been listening to music, because a stimulus to one or more senses during any trauma becomes locked in the negative engram with the memory of the trauma.

My patient remembered smelling the dressing on a salad that was in a container on her back seat. The container had opened during the impact with the other car.

"Think about where you got the salad," I said. After we worked through an energy balancing process, her hip felt fine and never bothered her again.

Later, I learned that she had met a man in a restaurant where she purchased the salad. The man had lived where she had also lived during a time when her marriage was failing.

The woman was replaying the memory of the marriage when the car accident occurred. Her body had healed everything except the emotions she experienced during her former marriage, which had become part of the new trauma's negative memory engram.

Memories are often interconnected. The smell of the salad was the catalyst that reawakened her memory of the conversation with the man in the restaurant and an earlier experience that was not yet resolved in her subconscious. An alarm bell began ringing at the restaurant, but the woman didn't hear it, and the emotions associated with her memory of a failed  marriage became subconsciously locked together with the car accident. Her body could heal completely *only after* the emotions associated with the earlier memory were addressed.

The alarms that we ignore, and the emotions associated with them, accumulate over time until one day, they produce physical, mental or emotional changes that become symptoms we finally recognize as a problem. Initial symptoms are often ignored. They may be subtle changes in sleep, food preferences, cravings, or even personality changes that others may notice and, hopefully, bring to our attention.

Drugs may help people feel better by changing symptom patterns, but the alarms that make symptoms necessary in the first place continue unanswered. Ultimately, therapies that don't address the source of the alarms are no more effective than putting a pillow over an alarm clock or disconnecting a warning light in your car.

> **You can never take enough medication or cut out enough organs to heal a negative memory engram.**

Survival and healing are mutually exclusive; they cannot operate simultaneously. Survival *always* takes precedence, until your lungs stop breathing and your heart

Survival ⟶ Healing

stops beating. Death comes, by whatever means, when your survival response itself is exhausted.

> Your body, which does not think, judge, or reason, will exhaust itself trying to survive both real and imagined emergencies – the alarm bells that you don't turn off – while healing is always ready and waits for your attention.

That was only the first step.

STEP TWO: **The experience that sounded the alarm is perceived subconsciously as an "ambush." You didn't see it coming and you couldn't have avoided it.**

Events that take you by surprise may be accompanied by thoughts such as, *"If only I had or hadn't done that or been there…,"* or *"I should or shouldn't have said that or done that…"*

> You can imagine how the young woman with seizures must have thought, *"If only I hadn't gone to that dentist,"* or, *"If I just hadn't gone to that second dentist"*; or even, *"People go to the dentist every day. How could this happen? I feel so stupid."*

These thoughts, as understandable as they may be, come from limiting, blaming, and ultimately destructive perspectives about yourself and your inherent worth, which you learned, mostly before you were seven years-old. They support a belief that in some way, you *deserve* the experiences you perceive as negative.

As you'll learn, unexpected things may happen and you may take "wrong turns," but none of these have to result in pain, illness, or dysfunction.

> **In fact, pain, illness, or dysfunction is actually the body's *solution*, not the problem! Your job is to discover what problem your body is solving!**

The steps of the *Heart, Soul and Spirit Cleanse,* which we'll explore in detail in the next chapter, are designed to identify and neutralize

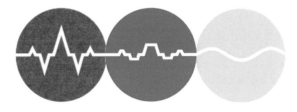

negative memory engrams, silence the original alarm(s), and allow your body's innate healing response to take over and progress rapidly, unhindered and unhampered. The results are often miraculous.

STEP THREE: Positive emotions *before* an ambush shift instantly to negative emotions *during* the experience. The shift *and* the emotions are *completely normal*, but you may not recognize or express them at the time, so they turn inward.

Ambushed positive feelings, which are present *before* an experience, and which we often forget, are far more important for healing than the negative emotions during and *after* an experience.

Once a positive emotion is "bushwhacked," like joy for instance, you may turn bitter, disappointed over the past, and afraid of future experiences. Anytime you begin to feel joy, you start "looking over your shoulder" for something else bad to happen. You may also try to control your circumstances and others around you, in an attempt to guard against future ambushes.

We call this an "allergy" to whatever positive feeling was involved. People will step back from a feeling of happiness, for example, because an unhealed negative memory engram alerts the subconscious to an "impending danger."

It's impossible, of course, to control everyone and everything around you, and you waste valuable time and energy, while resisting lots of other rich human experiences and relationships.

As important as it is to resolve negative feelings, *true* healing lies in resolving the wounded *positive* emotions that you were happily enjoying before the first alarm sounded!

More about this in the next chapter.

STEP FOUR: **Physical responses to the alarms – that is, *symptoms* – are a natural and necessary survival response.**

Pain is the most obvious symptom of all and it's a marvelously efficient way of getting us to pay attention to a likely injury. Without pain, we could bleed to death or walk around with broken bones.

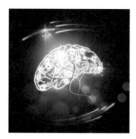

Some symptoms are uncomfortable, but not necessarily painful. Many come from a kind of "discharge" of ambushed positive feelings and unexpressed negative feelings, as explained in the story earlier of the young woman whose experience resulted in seizures.

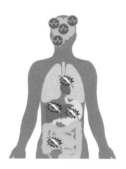

Any number of conditions may follow an unanswered alarm: colds, headache, fatigue, back pain, or a young father's bipolar behavior. Results may be debilitating like seizures, and even life-threatening, like the young woman with meningitis, or Dr. Hamer's cancer discovery. There are as many possibilities for symptoms as there are parts of the body and compartments in the brain!

In an effort to "control" or "cure" symptoms, many people fall into a seemingly endless pursuit of external treatments in a desperate search for true healing. But, as one of our mentors said . . .

> *"You can never treat enough symptoms to address the cause."*
> Dr. M.T. Morter, Jr.

In the next chapter, we'll go into the six steps to rapid healing.

Nutshells and Takeaways from Chapter 6

- Injury, illness *and* healing seem to progress as follows:
  - First in the **Spirit** – through your emotions;
  - Second, in your **Soul** (Mind) – through beliefs and memories;
  - Third, in your **Body** – through what we call symptoms.

- Your spirit is your *life* and there is no life without it.

- Your soul is the seat of your awareness, which ceases upon death.

- Your body is only along for the ride that starts in your spirit.

- Symptoms are simply responses that you can feel in your body.

- Symptoms result from *"timing problems"* due to trauma, toxicity, and your own thoughts, emotions and beliefs.

- A timing problem is any function in your body that occurs when it shouldn't, or doesn't occur when it should.

- Microorganisms (bacteria, yeast, or fungus, for example) are particles that already exist in all living organisms.

- Your habits create the environment inside your body for unfriendly organisms to proliferate or not.

- Germs don't cause disease; they are opportunists. The germ is nothing; the terrain is everything.

- Normal doesn't feel like anything, so it doesn't get our attention.

- Symptoms accompany experiences that we wish were different, but are unable to change at the time they occur.

- The memory of an experience can cause serious health trouble sooner or later.

- Pain, illness or dysfunction that continues after an emergency is over is due to *"negative memory engrams."*

- Engrams keep the memory of a trauma active in the subconscious as if the event were still happening.

- We tend to avoid the positive emotions that are "glued" to a negative memory engram.

- Memory is permanent, and every experience is recorded and cataloged with a sort of time stamp and intensity rating.

- Healing can only occur when a new message that the emergency is over reaches the same area of the brain as the original insult, and at the same intensity as the recorded memory.

- The laws of healing — as well as pain and disease — are universal.

- Healing often occurs beyond our ability to comprehend, let alone explain it.

- Stress is simply any stimulus that requires your body to change.

- Stress is neither good nor bad; in fact, it's essential for survival.

- How symptoms happen in four steps:
  1. Your "*Emergency*" mode is triggered by an "*alarm bell*" during an experience.
  2. The experience that sounded the alarm is perceived subconsciously as an "ambush." You didn't see it coming and, therefore, you couldn't have avoided it.
  3. Positive emotions *before* an ambush shift instantly to negative emotions *during* the experience.
  4. Physical responses to alarms – *symptoms* – are a natural and necessary survival response.

- Even the *perception* of stress can trigger an alarm.

- Survival takes priority over all else, including reason.

- We call stress-producing images in our minds, *"bears in the woods."*

- Bears are everywhere: spouse bears, work bears, kid bears, money bears.

- *"Adopting the right attitude can convert a negative stress into a positive one."* (Dr. Hans Selye)

- The emergency, *"fight-or-flight"* response is inborn, automatic, and necessary for survival.

- Positive emotions *before* an event happened are superseded by negative emotions that accompany and follow the event, which we may remember for the rest of our lives.

- Your body is designed to handle short term, real threats to survival that should last only seconds.

- Your body responds the same way to "bears" you think about as it does to real bears.

- Your body's systems can become exhausted fighting imaginary bears, until symptoms compel you to seek help.

- Alarms we ignore, and the emotions associated with them, accumulate over time until they produce symptoms that we recognize as a problem.

- Drugs help people feel better by changing symptom patterns, but the alarms that make symptoms necessary continue unanswered.

- You can never take enough medication or cut out enough organs to heal a negative memory engram.

- Pain, illness, or dysfunction is actually your body's *solution,* not the problem! Your job is to discover what problem your body is solving!

- Ambushed positive feelings *before* an experience are more important for healing than negative emotions during and *after* an experience.

- Once a positive emotion is "bushwhacked," you may become afraid of future experiences, and attempt to guard against future ambushes by trying to control circumstances and other people.

- You can never treat enough symptoms to address the cause.

Chapter 7

Six Steps to Rapid Healing

After you've made "friends with your symptoms," it's time to begin the healing process in earnest. Here are all six steps that are involved:

1. Recognize that an "ambush" occurred. Even when you can't recall what the ambush was, recognition itself begins to quiet the "alarm" almost instantly.
2. Evaluate your feelings after an ambush, as well as your emotional state before the experience occurred.
3. Change your mind, change your heart.
4. Release the past.
5. Receive your diploma...with honors!
6. Establish the continual, conscious exercise of your spirit.

Now let's examine each step in detail.

1. Recognize that an "ambush" occurred. Even when you can't recall what the ambush was, recognition itself begins to quiet the "alarm" almost instantly.

Experience has shown that alarms will continue to sound – and healing cannot occur fully – until you acknowledge three truths honestly in your heart:

> It Happened, It's Over, It's OK Now

Something that was beyond your conscious control turned on an alarm in the first place. *It isn't critical that you recall consciously what "it" was.* Many experiences occur at such a young age that conscious recall may be impossible, but the ambushes are stored in memory, and they can still be healed along with their effects.

When you look at your life, what else can you do besides acknowledge that "stuff" happened? You could go into "if-only land," if you like: *"if only I had or hadn't done or said such and such, how different would my life be?"* How productive is this, really, since clearly, *"it happened"* and it cannot *"un-happen"?*

A patient in the early weeks of my career said, *"I'm concerned about issues from my past life."* As empathetically as I could, I replied, *"I'm trying to help you in this life, so how about we deal with that first."*

The message that the emergency is over must be perceived in the same area of memory and with the same intensity as the original alarm.

It's time to trust again, like a turtle poking its head out of its shell. The coast is clear and it's safe to, *"come out and play!"*

Faith makes trusting easier. Without faith, life is a roulette wheel; it's a game plagued with uncertainty and risk. Faith in God contributes design and purpose to everything that happens, and removes the appearance of randomness and chance.

2. **Evaluate your feelings after an ambush, as well as your emotional state *before* the experience occurred.**

Take this in two steps:

Step 1: **Identify as many *negative* feelings as possible *following* the ambush.**

SAMPLE EMOTIONS TO "STIR THE POT"		
NEGATIVE EMOTIONS		
1. Embarrassed	29. Repulsive	57. Despair
2. Abused	30. Paranoia	58. Resignation
3. Ridicule	31. Unfaithful	59. Frustrated
4. Shame	32. Indignant	60. Persecuted
5. Guilt	33. Impatient	61. Envy
6. Bitterness	34. Rejected	62. Destructive
7. Regret	35. Rejecting	63. Unloved
8. Remorse	36. Irritated	64. Self-Pity
9. Anger	37. Cynical	65. Grief
10. Hate	38. Greed	66. Striving
11. Pride	39. Obsessed	67. Blame
12. Judgment	40. Powerless	68. Disgraced
13. Indecisive	41. Anxious	69. Worthless
14. Selfish	42. Spiteful	70. Humiliated
15. Depressed	43. Lonely	71. Apathy
16. Demanding	44. Concerned	72. Hostile
17. Immoral	45. Dominated	73. Tolerate
18. Critical	46. Jealous	74. Blame
19. Resentment	47. Grudge	75. Defilement
20. Vulnerable	48. Argumentative	76. Degradation
21. Abandoned	49. Compulsive	77. Loss
22. Suspicious	50. Fighting	78. Poverty
23. Worry	51. Ruthless	79. Manipulated
24. Fear	52. Submissive	80. Demeaned
25. Dishonest	53. Inadequate	81. Humiliation
26. Doubt	54. Devastated	82. Controlled
27. Bored	55. Indifferent	83. Betrayed
28. Upset	56. Dread	84. Denial

SAMPLE EMOTIONS TO "STIR THE POT"		
POSITIVE EMOTIONS		
1. Love	29. Conscientious	57. Loyal
2. Joy	30. Devoted	58. Comfort
3. Peace	31. Satisfied	59. Reliable
4. Patient	32. Gratified	60. Truthful
5. Kind	33. Honest	61. Eager
6. Faithful	34. Happy	62. Excited
7. Goodness	35. Calm	63. Respect
8. Gentle	36. Adoring	64. Compassion
9. Self-Control	37. Amiable	65. Pleased
10. Passion	38. Agreeable	66. Encouraged
11. Stable	39. Compatible	67. Understood
12. Trust	40. Expectant	68. Dependable
13. Careful	41. Right	69. Desire
14. Harmonious	42. Composure	70. Curious
15. Warm	43. Dedicated	71. Empathy
16. Glad	44. Serenity	72. Recognized
17. Intimacy	45. Quiet	73. Exhilaration
18. Friendship	46. Consistent	74. Holy
19. Perfection	47. Content	75. Innocent
20. Elated	48. Enjoyment	76. Clarity
21. Grateful	49. Fulfilled	77. Security
22. Tranquility	50. Cherish	78. Abundance
23. Delight	51. Desire	79. Restored
24. Creative	52. Sensitive	80. Purity
25. Accepting/Accepted	53. Imaginative	81. Celebrated
26. Inspired	54. Enthusiastic	82. Flow
27. Hopeful	55. Agreeable	83. Believe
28. Unwavering	56. Blissful	84. Faith

Charts adapted in part from the book *Feelings Buried Alive Never Die*, by Karol K. Truman

Note: The charts above are also found in Chapter 9, and may be downloaded from the links at ItsOK.WholeLifeWholeHealth.com.

Step 2: **Identify as many *positive* feelings as possible *before* the ambush.**

You don't have to *like* how an experience felt, and you don't have to volunteer for it again, but you must *acknowledge* it, and the feelings that accompanied and preceded it. This calms the unresolved emotions and begins to bring healing to your spirit, which is first in line to suffer any insult.

> Your emotional responses at the time an experience occurs are normal and usually appropriate; however, they no longer need to continue after the ambush is over.

The phenomenon of emotional shock is actually the absence of emotion. Most of us felt shock on September 11, 2001, when we witnessed the video report of airplanes crashing deliberately into the World Trade Center buildings in New York City and the Pentagon near Washington, D.C. We didn't know how to feel when these events occurred, because they had never happened before. With no memory to draw on of such an event – or even the possibility – we were left stunned.

The bombing of Pearl Harbor is another example of an unprecedented event being met with shock. The unthinkable happened and people were at a loss to grasp even the reality that played out before their very eyes.

It's important to realize that if you *could* have responded any other way to an event or a relationship, you *would* have, so no fair beating yourself up thinking you should have responded better! You did the best you could at the time, so relax and remember: *It Happened, It's Over, It's OK Now.*

3. Change your mind, change your heart.

This step is *critical* to free yourself from suffering in a *"victim prison"* of your own making, and to release yourself into *willing* participation in the highest purpose for your life.

Changing your mind from thoughts that deny your inherent worth into those that affirm it – and changing your heart from feelings that chain you to bitterness, resentment, anger, blame, etc., into those of acceptance and forgiveness – enables you to live in peace, joy and delight!

Changing your mind is the real meaning of the word, "repentance," in the Scriptures. Repentance simply requires that you accept responsibility for what you do, think and say, and turn from *de*structive to *con*structive patterns. The sooner you take ownership of your part in any circumstance or relationship, the sooner you'll graduate to something better!

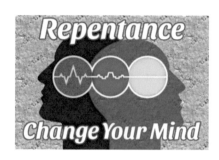

If repentance is changing your mind, then "forgiveness" is changing your heart. Forgiveness means, literally, to *"yield, concede, grant, relieve, exempt, or free,"* and it works two ways: You must forgive what you perceive as the wrongs committed

against you, and you must *receive* forgiveness for wrongs you have committed.

You have probably heard the cliché repeated many times, *"Forgive and forget";* however, memory is permanent, so forgetting is literally impossible.

Forgiving is your only option if you want to be free of past hurts, whether they happened 50 years, or five minutes ago.

- Forgiving *does not* require you to like, agree with, or excuse anything that happened to you, or that you have done.

- Forgiveness applies to others, to yourself, and even to God, because all three have been involved in the ambushes throughout your life.

- Forgiveness is simple, but not always easy, and absolutely necessary for healing.

> **Holding anything against anyone never affects them...**
> **it only makes *you* miserable!**

Here's how to forgive in four steps. Perform each step with feeling inside your own mind, and for your own freedom's sake!

First, *forgive everyone for everything.*

Line up everyone you've ever known across a huge stage and grant all pardon for everything. *Remember, this is for your sake, not theirs.* You'll be freeing yourself from all energy-wasting, forward progress-stopping resistance, resentment, and retaliation (even if it's silent and internal). If you think of particular individuals who have wronged you, pay special attention to forgiving them.

If anyone in history understood how important forgiveness is, it was Jesus! Even after being falsely accused, beaten, whipped, nailed to a cross, and left to die while suspended in the hot sun, He said, ***"Father forgive them, for they know not what they do"*** (Luke 23:24, ESV).

If anyone has ever had the right to hold a grudge, it was Jesus; instead, He prayed for those who had wronged Him, literally to death! Now *that's* an example worth following! It's also a comparison worth making, because Jesus was wronged more grievously than anyone could possibly wrong you or me.

Second, ***give everyone permission to forgive you.***

Even if you believe you were innocent in a situation, chances are that somewhere, sometime, you weren't. Give others permission to forgive you, to grant *you* amnesty and pardon for anything you *may* have done – a look, a word, or even just being in that place at that time.

Third, ***own your "stuff," repent, and forgive yourself.***

You've carried around the effects of the ambushes and the unanswered alarms in your body, soul (mind), and spirit long enough. Recognize, accept, and acknowledge where you missed the mark; then turn and choose a more excellent way.

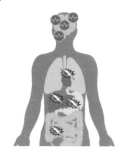

Fourth, ***forgive God***.

He can handle it. After all, He's the Architect of your life, and therefore, ultimately responsible for it. The operation of His purpose for your life may not feel good all the time, but God is ultimately loving and His purpose is ultimately good.

Religious tradition correctly teaches us to forgive others for what they do or what they have done. That's great, but it's incomplete, because it leaves out God's sovereignty. We are taught not to be angry at God when, in fact, as we discussed in the Introduction, God is the ultimate author of everything that happens everywhere, and this includes your own life.

> **"God … is operating all in all."** (1 Corinthians 12:6, CLNT)

If we fail to forgive God for what He allowed to happen – some of which, we would never allow in the lives of *our* children – we suppress what we intuitively know is just. The good news is that God *knows* that He is responsible (Read Psalm 139) and He provided a way for us to rightly forgive Him and make friends with Him, through what the Apostle Paul calls, *"the conciliation."*

> **"God was in Christ, conciliating the world to Himself, not reckoning their offenses to them … For Christ, then, are we ambassadors, as of God entreating through us. We are beseeching for Christ's sake, 'Be conciliated to God!'"**
> (2 Corinthians 5:19-20, CLNT)

 What is important for our discussion here is that *"conciliation"* is a description of one party – us – being estranged from God. Through Christ's sacrifice that canceled out any wrong we could ever do and removes any reason for us to remain estranged from the Father, He asks, in effect, *"Can we be friends now?"*

Why does this matter to your health?

Holding against God what you wish hadn't happened or wish had been different is the same as holding it against a person. Forgiving God is as

important as forgiving others for you to go free from your prison. Both can have serious consequences to your physical health, as much as your spiritual, mental and emotional well-being.

> If you're curious about "conciliation" and what the Bible *really* says, check out the book, *Rescuing God From the Rubble of Religion*.

Now, a couple quick notes:

1. You may never actually *speak* to *anyone*. This process is accomplished entirely within *yourself*, because that's where the alarm sounded in the first place.

2. This is serious business. The result is nothing short of your total freedom and release – spiritually, mentally, emotionally, and physically – from victim to victorious over the prison *you* built; a prison of resentment, bitterness, guilt, shame, disappointment, despair, blame, and more, all of which you can now walk away from...*FREE!*

4. Release the past.

Fill a box (figuratively speaking) with the experiences you wish hadn't happened or wish had been different. Throw anything in the box that no longer serves you, from your earliest childhood hurts to the most recent challenges. Whatever you no longer want to carry or drag behind you goes in the box.

Once the box is full, close the flaps, tape it up, or tie a bow around it, set it at God's feet and step back. This releases the burden of your past to the One Who can handle it.

To go free, simply "look God in the eye," and say, *"Thank You,"* for what you learned from your experiences and what you're learning now *(even if you don't know what it is!)*. At first, all you may be capable of is reciting this statement. As you apply the preceding steps, then, one day, you'll truly *feel* thankful.

> **"Come to Me, all who are weary and heavy-laden, and I will give you rest."** (Matthew 11:28, NASB)

When you fully recognize and appreciate the priceless jewels in your life today – the relationships and experiences that you wouldn't trade for anything, like the bipolar man's wife and daughters – you can truly say, *"Thank You"* to God for what His love and His purpose required, and feel genuinely glad for all that it cost you.

Write this down somewhere:

> **When your gratitude is greater than your pain, you'll be free. Then, healing becomes inevitable and unstoppable!**

5. Receive your diploma...with honors!

The first four steps of this process – recognition, repentance, forgiveness, and release with gratitude – transform experiences of pain, dishonor, or shame, into victories that qualify you for "graduation" with honors.

Another analogy we like to use is a military award ceremony, where God Himself pins a medal on your chest, like a warrior who has triumphed in battle.

In an athletic analogy, God hands you a trophy, which you are proud to receive and display in a place of prominence.

In all these images, the sources of our greatest shame, humiliation, or regret, suddenly become our greatest achievements. They are no longer memories to be buried and avoided, because they are all worthy of reverence and honor.

You're FREE! At last, you're on the "other side," living free, and living the victory! This applies not only to physical healing, but to healing in every area of life.

Now it's up to you to live, minute-by-minute and hour-by-hour, in ways that agree with, support, and reinforce your new "status," *no matter what anyone else says or does,* until it becomes integrated into the fabric of your character. You've moved from victim to victor and now it's time, as the Apostle Paul wrote to the Ephesians, ***"put on the new [humanity], created to be like God in true righteousness and holiness..."*** (Ephesians 4:24, NIV).

6. Establish the continual, conscious exercise of your spirit.

Sometimes, your life might feel like you're a passenger with no one at the wheel of your own vehicle. You have a "death grip" on the dashboard, as if your life is careening out of control.

You have an opportunity today to move into the driver's seat, with a *"life grip"* on the steering wheel, negotiating turns, highways and alleys, with greater and greater ease as your skills improve.

The most valuable instruments to guide us – like a spiritual *"GPS"* – are the Scriptures. Unique among the world's religious writings, the Scriptures – the Old and New Testaments – are, *"God speaking and revealing Himself to mankind,"* as Adlai Loudy described in his 1926 book, *God's Eonian Purpose.* Other religious writings, he said, are, *"man's attempt to explain his god."*

The principles contained in the Scriptures provide reliable road maps for daily health habits, including spiritual ones. As Barbara says, *"How are you going to pass this test called 'life' if you haven't read the book: the 'Basic Instructions Before Leaving Earth (the B.I.B.L.E.)?'"* If this seems like a bold, if not incredible statement, we've proved the Scriptures to be true in our own lives, and found God to be faithful, helping people restore and sustain their health and well-being, often contrary to conventional wisdom.

> Jesus said, ***"The spirit of truth will be guiding you into all the truth"*** (John 16:13, CLNT). What could be better than, *"all the truth"*?

Learning to be directed by the Holy Spirit has proven 100 percent successful in providing a foundation for levels of peace and ease that translate into *"Living the Victory,"* in profound physical and mental health and well-being.

The more you remind yourself of who you are to God, according to His own word, the more grateful you become for everyone and everything that has been or is today a part of your life. The more you guard this awareness, the more alert you will be when "alarm bells" sound; you will hear them sooner and act on them quicker.

You become more loving, accepting, and forgiving of yourself and others. You discover how those qualities improve your physical, mental, and emotional health, and also your relationships at home, at work, and at play.

In time, you may even learn possibly the best lesson in preventive health care: *"**Do not judge so that you will not be judged**"* (Matthew 7:1, NASB). Repent, forgive, bless, and go on.

Feeling truly grateful can drill right through many of the *Six Steps to Rapid Healing*, so don't forget the shortcut from Chapter 5!

Nutshells and Takeaways from Chapter 7

- Six steps to rapid healing:

  1. Recognize that an "ambush" occurred.
     - It Happened, It's Over, It's OK Now.

  2. Evaluate your feelings before and after an "ambush."

- Identify *negative* feelings *following* an ambush.
- Identify *positive* feelings *before* an ambush.

  3. Change your mind, change your heart. Free yourself from suffering in a *"victim prison"* of your own making.

4. Release the past.

5. Receive your diploma.

6. Establish the continual, conscious exercise of your spirit.

- Faith makes trusting easier.

- Without faith, life is a game plagued with uncertainty and risk.

- Faith in God contributes design and purpose to everything that happens.

- Shock is actually the absence of emotion.

- If you *could* have responded any other way to any event or relationship, you *would* have.

- "Repentance" means changing your mind.

- "Forgiveness" is changing your heart.

- Forgive in 4 steps:

  1. Forgive everyone for everything.
  2. Give everyone permission to forgive you.
  3. Own your "stuff," repent, and forgive yourself.
  4. Forgive God.

- Forgetting is virtually impossible. Forgiving is your only option.

- Holding anything against anyone never affects them...it only makes *you* miserable!

- Holding against God what you wish hadn't happened or wish had been different is the same as holding it against a person.

- Beyond winning our forgiveness or pardon, Christ died to win our "*conciliation*" to God.

- Christ's death and resurrection removed any reason for us to be angry with God, or afraid of Him.

- Look God in the eye and say, "*Thank You,*" for what you learned from your experiences and what you're learning now (*even if you don't know what it is!*).

- When your gratitude is greater than your pain, you'll be free; then healing becomes inevitable and unstoppable!

- Your worst experiences are actually medals of honor pinned to the chest of a soldier who triumphed in battle. They are trophies worthy of a place of honor. You've earned your diploma!

- Use the Scriptures like a spiritual GPS.

- The Scriptures are, *"God speaking and revealing Himself to mankind,"* while other religious writings are, *"man's attempt to explain his god."* (Adlai Loudy, "God's Eonian Purpose," 1926)

- The Bible is *"Basic Instructions Before Leaving Earth,"* and contains reliable road maps for daily health habits, including spiritual ones.

- *"How are you going to pass this test called 'life' if you haven't read the book?"* (Barbara Brown, MSE)

- Learning to be directed by the Holy Spirit has proven 100 percent successful.

- Jesus said, ***"The spirit of truth will be guiding you into all the truth"*** (John 16:13, CLNT). What could be better than, *"all the truth"*?

- The more you remind yourself of who you are to God, the more grateful you become for everyone and everything that has been a part of your life.

- The more you guard this awareness, the more alert you will be when "alarm bells" sound, and the quicker you'll act on them.

- The best lesson in preventive health care: ***"Do not judge so that you will not be judged"*** (Matthew 7:1, NASB). Repent, forgive, bless, and go on.

The sources of our greatest shame, humiliation, or regret
are no longer memories to be buried and avoided;
rather, they are all worthy of reverence and honor.

Chapter 8

Put the Steps Together

Let's go through all the steps of the *Heart, Soul and Spirit Cleanse* in one fluid sequence, from the original insult through healing.

First, the insult occurs

1. An "*alarm bell*" sounds in your spirit during an experience.

2. The experience is perceived subconsciously as an "ambush."

3. Positive emotions *before* an ambush turn to negative emotions *during* the experience, and stay that way until you resolve them.

4. Physical symptoms are a *survival response* — a kind of "discharge" of ambushed positive feelings and unresolved negative feelings.

Next, take Six Steps to Rapid Healing

1. *"It Happened!"* – Recognize that an "ambush" occurred, even if you can't recall what it was.

2. Identify as many *negative* emotions as possible *when* the "ambush" occurred, and as many *positive* emotions as possible *before* it happened. (For help identifying specific emotions, download the charts from the online resource.)

3. *"It's Over!"* – Repent, forgive, bless, and go on. Changing your mind from past thoughts, beliefs and actions is

critical! Then, freely forgive others, including yourself and God. Give others permission to forgive you, even when you think you did nothing that needs forgiveness.

4. **"It's OK Now!"** – Fill a box with the experiences you wish hadn't happened or wish had been different, and place it at God's feet. Say, *"Thank You for what I learned and what I am learning. Thank you for what Your love and Your purpose for me required."* When this step is heartfelt, and when you can acknowledge in your heart that the "jewels" in your life today made every step of your past worthwhile, you're free!

5. Receive your "graduation diploma." Well done!

6. Establish the continual, conscious exercise of your spirit; the single most important step to sustain optimal overall health and well-being.

Review and repeat these steps as often as necessary. Experiences you wish were different are likely to happen again, and memories of past events and relationships are likely to surface.

You can achieve healthier responses to future "ambushes" by using the ten steps we just outlined to maintain a healthy perspective, release any ill effects, and promote maximum spiritual, mental, and physical well-being.

> Don't forget the shortcut to all this in Chapter Five: *"In all things be giving thanks ..."* In other words, *get grateful or get sick!*

Permanent healing seems to depend on your willingness to recognize and receive the miracles happening in and around your life all the time. Sometimes, the miracles you want aren't the ones you most need to recognize and receive first. The simple fact is, however, the more you look, the more you'll find; the more you find, the more there are to discover. It's a skill you can develop.

Recognizing and receiving miracles results in an unshakable confidence in your true worth, and a constant state of appreciation, wonder, reverence, and even a sense of worship.

Barbara was once the Keynote Speaker for a world convention in Abuja, Nigeria, and after she spoke, she invited people to come forward for prayer. The crowd that was gathered in front of the stage pushed a 17 year-old boy forward. He was blind from birth and known to many who had come hoping for his miracle. The boy's eyeballs were pure white ...no cornea, iris, or pupil.

As Barbara laid her hands on the boy, praying for him in the name of Jesus, *the boy's eyes began to form and he saw for the first time in his life!*

Barbara asked the boy, *"What do you see?"*

He replied, *"I see shapes! I see fingers! I see you!"*

"How do you feel?" Barbara asked.

"I feel happy," he smiled.

The stadium erupted in spontaneous praise and worship.

How do you explain a boy born blind suddenly receiving normal eyeballs and the gift of sight to go with them? God created something out of nothing that night, so don't dismiss the possibility of miraculous healing in your own life.

> *"With men it is impossible,"* Jesus said, *"but not with God, for all is possible with God."* (Mark 10:27, CLNT)

The truth is, you can live in the *Realm of the Miraculous*!

"Yeah, but Doc," I can hear the question now, *"This doesn't work for everybody, right?"*

We all know people who do everything they can, including praying constantly, but they never get well.

Why?

Here are some possibilities:

Five Reasons Why Healing May Be Elusive or Short-lived.

First, let's list the reasons, and then we'll go into them in detail.

1. Someone may have more invested in their condition than in healing.
2. They may have more invested in pleasing others than in being healthy.
3. There is a higher "**Top Priority**" for healing.
4. There is an ongoing stimulus that interferes with healing.
5. Their "infirmity" serves a higher purpose.

1. **Someone may have more invested in their condition than in healing.**

Some people will actually reject healing in favor of pain, illness, or dysfunction. They fear losing the attention they get from being sick *more* than they value healing. I know it seems unbelievable, but we've worked with clients who were within reach of a real breakthrough, and who chose to reject it.

Here are a few examples:

> A woman rushed up to the stage after a workshop, and *proudly* listed her conditions and medications, smiling the whole time, as if she were showing pictures of her grandkids! The principles we had shared that night had fallen on deaf ears.

> A client who had suffered debilitating headaches every day for 40 years experienced total healing in six weeks. He stopped coming because, he said, *"I just can't believe they can be gone that easily."* His headaches returned, fulfilling his belief.

Can you imagine preferring a headache that woke you up at 4 am and put you to bed at 4 pm every day for 40 years?! I can't imagine having a headache for four minutes, never mind 40 years! It still baffles me today.

> Another client, who had improved rapidly, announced that she could not continue, because, she said, *"If I get any better, my husband will stop doing everything for me."*

The healing power within you works best when you accept it and adopt a spirit of gratitude for its perfection. When the personal "payoff" of infirmity – *better known as self-pity* – is greater than the perceived benefit of healing, some may deny themselves the opportunity to heal and reject even the possibility of experiencing a miracle.

2. **Someone has more invested in pleasing others than in being healthy.**

Your health is entirely your choice, but when well-meaning family and friends give advice freely, believing that they are *"just trying to help,"* the result can sometimes be tragic.

Here's just one example:

A colleague and friend, with as healthy a lifestyle as anyone I knew, once asked for help with life-threatening esophageal cancer. By the time we began working together, she had been under medical care for months, with a poor prognosis for recovery.

We quickly identified the insult that started the "alarm," and, using the *Heart, Soul and Spirit Cleanse,* she began to improve immediately. Her appetite returned, and she gained strength and stamina over a few short weeks, even while continuing conventional drug therapy. She even began planning to return to work. Following a visit from her parents and sisters, however, my friend's condition deteriorated rapidly. It was as if her celebration of renewed strength and vitality had been swept out from underneath her feet.

The conflict inside her was obvious when I saw my friend for what proved to be the last time. Without speaking a word, I could see that she had resigned herself to follow her family's wishes that she continue with chemotherapy, which had only served to weaken her before.

The miracle that had been operating powerfully stopped abruptly and she died a few weeks later.

If you care more about making *others* feel better than you do about being *well*, you run the risk of turning your back on a miracle. Pleasing others may cost you more than you would ever want to pay, so when you face a choice between trusting God and pleasing people, trust God.

Even if no one in your life welcomes the healing miracle you experience, guard it. As the Apostle Paul wrote in 1 Timothy 6:20, *"...that which is committed to you, guard"* (CLNT).

When Barbara's body was ravaged by muscular dystrophy, she prayed for God's purpose – rather than her own – to be fulfilled in her life. Until then, she had no motivation to pray like that, much less expect to hear the Lord's voice weeks later, when He said, *"Start walking."* God permanently healed Barbara for His purpose and she's a walking miracle today. Her story has inspired audiences all over the world, lifting them to see beyond their current conditions and receive their miracles too.

Do you think that Barbara would let anyone or anything steal her miracle? Not a chance! No one can tell her that cripples don't walk.

Someone with an opinion will always be at the mercy of someone with an experience.

Opinion vs. Experience

3. There is a higher, Top Priority for healing.

Bodies heal according to internal priorities that may not match your conscious "checklist." Healing doesn't always begin where you want it to, but rather, in the area of the greatest immediate threat to your survival.

Here's an example of Top Priority:

A 90 year-old man with painful hands and wrists, thought he had carpal tunnel syndrome. After working with him for two weeks, he reported no change; "But," he said, "I can go up and down stairs without knee pain now." He hadn't said anything about a knee problem and I never touched his knees!

The man's body worked to heal his knees first, because they were more important to his immediate survival than his hands and wrists.

> **Just remember: *"Trust the process."***

Skeptics sometimes voice a paradigm called, *"the limitation of matter."* The premise is that healing is subject to certain physical limitations. Under this belief, the boy in Nigeria would never  have received his sight. The 70 year-old man whose neck appeared fused with arthritis on X-rays would never have regained his flexibility. The woman with rods implanted alongside her spinal column would never have enjoyed hiking mountains again. The woman whose rotator cuff muscles had been literally torn from their attachments, would never have trimmed her hedges that summer.

Healing is often a process, not an instantaneous arrival at a destination. Either way, however, healing is inevitable when interference with its normal expression has been removed. Beliefs have more to do with your well-being than you often realize. Experiences like the ones I've related already have convinced Barbara Brown and me never to place limits on your God-given healing potential.

4. An ongoing stimulus interferes with healing.

The doctor who first inspired me to become a wellness doc once told me, *"If you leave my office and eat a hamburger, or get mad at someone on the way home, you'll undo all the good we just did."* In other words, when healing stops or never seems to begin, and you've eliminated the three possibilities we've already examined, look at what *you're* doing to interfere with the process. Don't conclude that you're defective or unlucky.

This principle is similar to Top Priority, in that your choices in some area or areas of life are creating a greater survival priority than healing.

The most common question Barbara and I hear when we finish our first meeting with someone, who has just caught a glimpse of the possibilities of total healing is, ***"How long will this last?"***

Our answer is, *"It's up to you. Your body will respond perfectly to the choices you make. If you do everything you've always done, you'll get what you've always had. If, however, you make a spiritual commitment to yourself; if you take ownership of the only body and the only life God gave you, and commit to serving the highest purpose for your life in every area, you can walk in divine health."*

Your choices ultimately determine the course and speed of healing. When healing isn't happening, examine your choices first.

5. Infirmity serves a higher purpose.

The phenomenon of an infirmity serving a higher purpose requires a leap of faith to accept. We've rarely witnessed it, but the phenomenon does have precedent.

> A man was troubled for many years by a condition for which he never found relief. He called the problem a *"splinter in the flesh,"* and as a man of great faith, he prayed three times to have the "splinter" removed. The Lord Himself told the man that His grace was enough, so he wore it as a badge of honor. People would have to look past his appearance to hear the message that Paul of Tarsus brought *(2 Corinthians 12)*.

> Another man was merely plain-looking, but people rejected and despised him. He was said to be a man of suffering, familiar with pain, and seemingly afflicted by God; but his message was compelling, convicting, and promising, all at the same time. He was eventually killed for what he shared throughout his country. His life and teachings are still studied and even followed by billions of people worldwide. His name was Jesus of Nazareth *(Isaiah 53)*.

It should be obvious from the two examples above that infirmity which serves a higher purpose is extremely rare.

In the next chapter, you'll find a tool to identify *your* Top Priorities and the emotions that got you into trouble in the first place.

Nutshells and Takeaways from Chapter 8

- The *Heart, Soul and Spirit Cleanse* in sequence:

  - The insult occurs
    1. An *"alarm bell"* sounds in your spirit.
    2. An "ambush" is perceived.
    3. Positive emotions turn to negative emotions.
    4. Symptoms are a *survival response.*

  - Six Steps to Rapid Healing

    1. *"It Happened!"* – Recognize the "ambush."
    2. Identify *positive* emotions *before* the "ambush" and *negative* emotions *when* it occurred.
    3. *"It's Over!"* – Repent, forgive, bless, and go on.
    4. *"It's OK Now!"* – Say, *"Thank You"* and acknowledge the "jewels" in your life today.
    5. Receive your "graduation diploma."
    6. Exercise your spirit daily.

- Don't forget the shortcut: ***"In all things be giving thanks ..."***

- Recognizing and receiving miracles results in unshakable confidence.

- You can live in the *Realm of the Miraculous*!

- Five Reasons Why Healing May Be Elusive:

  1. Someone may have more invested in their condition than in healing.
  2. Someone may have more invested in pleasing others than in being healthy.
  3. There is a higher *"Top Priority"* for healing.
  4. There is an ongoing stimulus that interferes with healing.
  5. The *"infirmity"* serves a higher purpose.

- Pleasing others may cost you more than you would ever want to pay.

- When you face a choice between trusting God and pleasing people, trust God.

- Guard your miracles: **"...that which is committed to you, guard."** (1 Timothy 6:20, CLNT)

- Someone with an opinion will always be at the mercy of someone with an experience.

- Bodies heal according to internal survival priorities.

- Healing is a process, not a destination.

- Healing is inevitable when interference with its normal expression has been removed.

- Your choices ultimately determine the course and speed of healing.

- When healing isn't happening, examine your choices first.

- Infirmity that serves a higher purpose is exceedingly rare. Don't look there first.

Chapter 9

What In the World Happened to Me?

Your body is metaphorical about how it breaks down. In other words, symptoms occurring in certain parts of your body can provide valuable clues about why the symptoms are happening. These clues can steer you toward resolving the problem, so healing can begin.

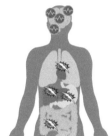

Many books have been written by alternative heath gurus that try to link illnesses, or pain in certain body parts, to specific emotions. Our experience is that every person's perception of a situation or relationship is so different, that these kinds of interpretations don't always hit the mark and may even be misleading.

Pairing symptoms with metaphors from the examples we've shared in this book already, plus some other stories, may help you resolve conditions quickly. The examples we share below aren't necessarily applicable to everyone, but they come from our experience helping real people heal.

- **Meningitis:** The first symptom that appeared was a *sore throat*. This is a clue that the person *wanted to scream or say something, but didn't or couldn't.* When I suggested the connection to the mother, she knew immediately what had happened.

LESSON: Don't ignore symptoms; they are your body's mechanism to signal that something needs your attention. Recognize symptoms quickly and go to work to identify the stimulus and the emotion(s) surrounding them.

- **Seizures:** No symptoms preceded the first seizure in a dentist's office. The fact that the actual stimulus occurred a week earlier made it clear that the seizures were a ***violent energy discharge after a week of feeling disrespected and unable to express it***. The only reason that seizures continued for 18 months was that everyone, including the patient, was focused on the wrong dental visit.

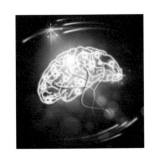

> **LESSON:** Don't think you're crazy just because everyone else is baffled by your condition. If you feel suspicious of the diagnosis or treatment proposed, get more opinions and don't stop until you find someone who thinks differently and who makes sense to you.

- **Hip pain:** The patient was ***stopped in her forward progress***, literally and figuratively.

> **LESSON:** Find the primary stimulus. Symptoms that linger after most others have resolved indicates that the primary stimulus hasn't yet been identified.

- **Muscular Dystrophy:** Here we see something modeled in front of someone throughout her childhood. Barbara saw her dad, a World War II Marine veteran, and her aunt both wither to death with a crippling disease. Doctors told the family it would affect two of the four kids and Barbara prayed to be the only one, so the others could be spared. ***Her body fulfilled her prayer and manifested the images she observed in her dad every day of her most formative years.***

> **LESSON:** *Watch what you pray for. Even if you pray NOT to get sick, the images you dwell on will contain sickness, not health.* Pray to fulfill the purpose for which you were created with robust health and those images will dominate your imagination. Such images don't guarantee a positive outcome, but at least they won't add interference with the innate healing response.

- **Headache:** First, make sure you are well-hydrated; drink water. Then, ***think about what you are dwelling on mentally that you find worrying or troubling.***

- **Eyes:** What is it that you ***don't want to look*** at, or ***don't want to see***?

- **Ears:** What is it that you ***don't want to hear***, or ***to what/whom do you not want to listen***?

- **Nose:** I don't think that Barbara or I have ever run into a problem with a sense of smell. That said, if it were to show up, I'd ***look for a highly charged event or encounter while a distinctive smell was in the air.***

- **Throat:** What are you ***holding back from saying or screaming***, as in the case of a sore throat that became meningitis?

- **Neck:** Neck pain seems to be where anger manifests. ***What are you angry about, or with whom are you angry?***

- **Shoulders:** The cliché about ***"shouldering responsibilities"*** is particularly appropriate, because those kinds of feelings seem to settle on or in the shoulders.

- **Shoulder blades/upper back:** Look for what you have **_trouble tolerating_** or what you can **_no longer tolerate_**.

- **Low back:** When you feel a **_loss of support_**, you may experience low back weakness or pain.

- **Upper Legs:** What are you **_trying to run from, but can't get away from_**, literally or figuratively?

- **Knees:** What seems to be, "**_cutting you off at the knees_**." Also look for a **_feeling of fear_**, however subtle it may be.

> **NOTE:** _Achy or weak knees are also signs of adrenal fatigue or adrenal exhaustion._ The adrenal glands are the stress glands, so look for a persistent stress that you find wearying.
>
> **BEWARE:** _Thyroid trouble is most often adrenal exhaustion_ that has gone unaddressed. Medical tests are most often geared toward the thyroid gland. Every client we've ever seen with supposed thyroid trouble improved dramatically when we addressed the stresses to which the _adrenal_ glands were responding.

- **Lower legs/feet:** Look for what you **_"can't stand."_** A colleague's patient with painful boils on his feet had watched his house burn to the ground, a sight he literally could not stand. (He might just as easily have gone blind!)

- **Right side:** In Chinese medicine, the right side of the body contains or expresses more **_female energy; i.e, nurturing, creative, caring, allowing_**. When conditions appear on the right side of the body, you may be **_dealing with more female energy, or having to express more of it, contrary to your usual personality or preference._**

- **Left Side:** In Chinese medicine, the left side of the body contains or expresses more *male energy; i.e, discipline, calculating, dominating, insistent*. When conditions appear on the left side of the body, you may be *dealing with more male energy, or having to express more of it, contrary to your usual personality or preference.*

In the case of the young woman with left hip pain that persisted after other symptoms from her car accident had resolved, male energy was certainly involved in her failed marriage, of which she was reminded just before the car accident.

- **Heart:** Who is *hurting, has hurt, or has broken your heart?* Who do you *want to love*, but may be *unable to express it?*

- **Lungs:** Where in your life do you *feel suffocated?*

- **Stomach, Digestion, Elimination:** *Mental and emotional stresses will abruptly stop digestion.* Emergency survival responses take priority over digestion, rest, and healing, all of which are governed by the same part of your autonomic nervous system.

A new patient arrived with a digestive tract so sensitive that she experienced terrible pain and diarrhea when she ate *anything*. She had been diagnosed with Crohn's disease and was facing surgery to remove a section of "diseased" colon. We worked together only a few times to identify the emotions that had been ambushed some years earlier.

She came in one day ecstatic, because she had eaten some potato chips just to see what would happen.

She was thrilled to suffer no ill effects at all. She began experimenting with other foods and worked her way up to a normal diet. She also postponed the surgery indefinitely.

- **Bipolar, Obsessive/Compulsive, Multiple Personality, and other mental "disorders":** When these conditions are metaphorical, we have to *look for what a person doesn't like or is avoiding within themselves*. Often,  however, these kinds of conditions seem to result from *"mimicking" behavior* observed in someone whose love is treasured and whose approval is craved at a most vulnerable time of life. It's also possible that during the same vulnerable time of life, the person found it impossible to deal with behavior in parents or caretakers (usually), and *coped by likewise developing bizarre behaviors.*

- **Children:** When children have a health challenge, from birth to puberty, they are often responding to a *stress that the mother is experiencing*. The younger the child, the more immediate and direct the effects will be.

Kids are conceived, develop and grow in the envelope of their mothers' energy field. Emotional stress in a mother's life transfers to the child and illness may develop quickly. If Mom becomes agitated, her child may develop a rash, develop a fever, or stop eating, for example.

A young mother brought her three month-old son to the office, because he had not passed stool from the time he was three weeks old. He didn't look sickly, but his mother was understandably concerned. The child's pediatrician told her, "He's just using it."

Thankfully, that answer didn't satisfy her.

When the mother told me about the pediatrician's assessment, I asked, "Using what? It's waste!"

Three energy-balancing procedures later and the child's condition was unchanged. Time for Mom to get checked. After three visits with the mother, there was still no change in the child. Whatever stress the little boy was responding to involved more family members than usual!

Mom brought the baby's two sisters in (elementary and junior high school-age). Again, there was no change in the child after three office visits.

Finally we brought in Dad, Mom, two sisters and the infant. I told the family that the baby was responding to a stress that must have been pretty big to affect the whole family. Something happened within days of when the child was three weeks old. I checked the child first, but he was clear and all the signs pointed to Dad. After the child's father was balanced, the child began passing stool within a few hours. "It's like he's making up for lost time," the mother told me the next day on the phone. She also shared what the stress was that they had all "forgotten" about when the baby was three weeks old, "to the day."

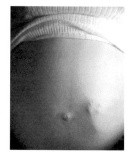

Kids, especially infants, are sponges. They feel whatever Mom feels, even in the womb. A baby's health may not *always* reflect an emotional stress that Mom is experiencing, but any stress that Mom is going through will affect her child. If the mother's stress is great enough during her pregnancy, the child's development may be affected. The results can range widely from temperament or sleep trouble, to disastrous disabilities with lifelong effects.

A mother carried her 10 year-old daughter into the office. The child was nonverbal; her arms and hands were frozen in a flexed position, her legs were almost as thin as her arms, and her body overall was about the size of a six year-old.

The best we could do was to help the child feel more comfortable and gain some movement in her arms.

The mother shared a heart-wrenching story of her terribly abusive marriage, and an unwanted pregnancy that was plagued with difficulty from beginning to end. The young girl died about a year after we'd first seen her and it was a blessing.

All of the examples we have just examined are demonstrations of how our emotions create energy frequencies, or vibrations, that the cells in our organs and tissues respond to, which we

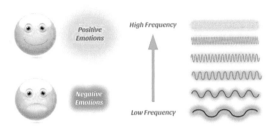

experience as symptoms. In this way, our bodies become a kind of "read-out" that can help us pinpoint the cause of the distress that has led to our *"dis-ease,"* which can progress to a disease.

Once again, we can see how treating a disease, while helping us feel better, does nothing to address the cause. The good news is that you now know how to go beyond treatment by healing your mind, memory and emotions.

> Ultimately you are changing your "vibrations" to make illness unnecessary to continue, or to prevent disease from occurring in the first place.

Quick guidelines to stop illness in its tracks:

At the first sign of a symptom, *STOP* and *THINK:*

- Where am I? (or where was I?)
- Who is/was around me?
- What is/was going on at the time?
- What was I doing?
- What was I thinking and feeling?

The quicker you identify these factors, the quicker you'll make symptoms unnecessary to continue.

Become a mature observer of your emotions, rather than their hapless victim.

Emotions are, literally, *"energy-in-motion."* They can be triggered in a microsecond by different and often familiar stimuli. Emotions are recalled from subconscious memory faster than you can grab hold of them, let alone stop them.

Emotion: "Energy in Motion"

> As *energy-in-motion* coming from memory, emotions will change, even in the midst of an experience ... just watch.

Here are some examples of various emotional stimuli:

- **Tones of voice** – We recognize the sound of hostility, anger, or love in someone's voice, and we respond to each emotion according to our memories of similar experiences. We can even *recall* a tone of voice without hearing it physically, but our emotions may respond as if we were in an actual experience.

- **Sounds** – Banging, beeping, engines, trains, etc., can evoke our memory of similar sounds.

- **Specific words** – Words can affect us deeply and the younger we are, the truer this is. Whether you hear, "You're pathetic," or, "You're brilliant" enough times over a long enough period of time, they feel normal, but they have very different consequences later in life.

- **Looks** – Looks are like silent words; whole pronouncements can be conveyed in a glance. We learn what certain looks in our parents' eyes mean when we are tiny kids. When we see the same looks in other people's eyes, the feelings we had as kids can spring up, even when we're adults.

- **Times** – Anniversaries, holidays, and even seasons can evoke emotional memories. Thanksgiving, for example, is full of smells, tastes and family traditions that stretch across generations. Memories of such powerful experiences and positive emotions are wonderful. Too often, however, memory seems to work the other way.

Here's an important principle to remember:

> **Situations themselves are neutral;**
> **they are not positive or negative.**

We assign meaning and value to situations through our emotions, which we interpret or perceive as positive or negative, based on our memories of similar sensory stimuli.

You can develop the ability to recognize emotions, rather than be carried away by them. When you develop this skill, you become an observer of an experience, rather than a victim of your own emotions.

Try this the next time your emotions are triggered suddenly:

- Observe the emotions as they arise and allow them to move through you.
- Don't resist the feelings, but don't give voice to them. Nothing fuels an argument faster than two emotionally uncontrolled people.
- Realize that the experience of your emotions is how memory "feels."
- Ask yourself this question: *"What do I need to learn here?"* or, *"What can I learn from this that could help me?"*

Barbara Brown and I have had lots of practice with this process in different relationships since the mid-1990's. The experience of being the observer of your own emotions is one of the most helpful skills to develop.

> **Both parties have different communication styles based on background, upbringing, and conditioning.**

When you *observe* your emotions rather than be *carried off* by them, you can accept someone, because they may be communicating in the only way they know how. Everyone may be doing the best they can, given their conditioning. You don't have to *like* them or how they act, but you can *accept* them without *agreeing* or *condoning*, and without *judging* them as right or wrong. Whether you include them in your life at all is entirely up to you.

You'll soon discover that arguments can stop and the tone can change quickly when one person is no longer "playing the game." You may even discover that your relationship with the other person improves as you develop the skill to observe and stand above your emotions, rather than participating from a low level in a no-win confrontation.

Acceptance, like forgiveness, is all about setting *you* free. You can allow yourself to *learn* from your experiences, rather than be destroyed by them.

Acceptance is the essence of *"It Happened, It's Over, It's OK Now."*

Nutshells and Takeaways from Chapter 9

- Your body is metaphorical about how it breaks down.

- Don't ignore symptoms! They are your body's way of telling you that something needs your attention.

- Don't think you're crazy just because everyone else is baffled by your condition.

- Don't pray NOT to get sick! The images you dwell on will contain sickness, not health.

NOTE: The examples below are observations *ONLY*. They do not necessarily apply to you.

Symptom/Condition	Metaphor
Sore throat	Want to scream or say something but don't or can't
Seizures	Violent energy discharge – this case happened after feeling disrespected and unable to express it
Hip pain	Forward progress is stopped
Muscular Dystrophy	Determination to spare others
Headache	Dehydration, worry or concern
Eyes/Vision	What you don't want to look at or see
Ears/Hearing	What you don't want to listen to or hear
Nose/Smell	Highly charged situation while a distinctive smell was in the air
Neck pain	Anger
Shoulder pain	"Shouldering" responsibilities for others
Shoulder blade area pain	Tolerance/Can't tolerate
Low back ache or pain	Loss of support, gradual or sudden
Upper legs	Running from something, but unsuccessful
Knees*	Fear, or cut off at the knees. *May also be adrenal fatigue/exhaustion from

	wearying stress, often misdiagnosed as thyroid trouble
Right side	Female energy: nurturing, creative, caring, allowing
Left side	Male energy: discipline, calculating, dominating, insistent
Heart	Who hurt you/broke your heart? Can't express desire for love
Lungs	Feeling suffocated
Stomach, digestion, elimination	Any mental or emotional stress can interfere
Mental disorders	Mimicking behavior in others, avoiding something within oneself
Children	Reflecting mother's stress from conception forward

(The chart above is available as a download from ItsOK.WholeLifeWholeHealth.com.)

- Kids, especially infants, are sponges. They feel whatever Mom feels, even in the womb.

- The quicker you identify symptoms, the quicker you'll make them unnecessary.

- At the first sign of a symptom, *STOP* and *THINK:*

  - Where am I? (Or, where was I when I first noticed a symptom?)
  - Who is/was around me?
  - What is/was going on at the time?

- What was I thinking before the symptom started?
- What was I feeling before the symptom started?

- Emotions are *"energy-in-motion."*

- Become the observer of your emotions, rather than the victim.

- Examples of emotional stimuli:
  - Tones of voice
  - Sounds
  - Specific words

- Looks
- Times – anniversaries, holidays, etc.

- Situations are neutral; they are not positive or negative.

- In any situation, ask yourself, *"What do I need to learn here?"* or, *"What can I learn from this that could help me?"*

- You can accept without agreeing and without judging.

You can't change or "un-live" an event that happened 50 years ago or five minutes ago.

They're both over and healing is waiting for you here and now.

Chapter 10

How to Identify Your Top Priorities

and the emotions that got you into trouble

Whether it's getting rid of headaches or improving relationships, we've provided a simple form on the web page for this book. Download it to help stimulate and focus your thinking, activate your memory, and help you determine clearly the top priorities for what you most want to work better in your life.

Once you identify your priorities, download the charts of emotions below. Apply the steps from the last three chapters to identify and remove any interference between you and the innate healing potential that God created in you, or take the shortcut in Chapter 5!

Dating these forms is a great way to track your success!

How to identify your Top Priorities

- **Pick your Top 3 Health Challenges** (these can be physical, mental, emotional or spiritual)
  - Example: Seizures

- **When did each of these begin?**
  - Example: Seizures started 18 months ago

- **What major event happened in your life at that time?**
  - Example: Dental visit – Dr. and assistant were pre-occupied during procedure

- **What negative feeling(s) do you associate with that event?**
  - Example: Neglected, angry, frustrated, impatient

- **What positive feeling(s) do you recognize prior to that event?**
  - Example: Happy, expectant, hopeful, relaxed

Here again are the charts of emotions found in Chapter 7:

SAMPLE EMOTIONS TO "STIR THE POT"		
NEGATIVE EMOTIONS		
1. Embarrassed	29. Repulsive	57. Despair
2. Abused	30. Paranoia	58. Resignation
3. Ridicule	31. Unfaithful	59. Frustrated
4. Shame	32. Indignant	60. Persecuted
5. Guilt	33. Impatient	61. Envy
6. Bitterness	34. Rejected	62. Destructive
7. Regret	35. Rejecting	63. Unloved
8. Remorse	36. Irritated	64. Self-Pity
9. Anger	37. Cynical	65. Grief
10. Hate	38. Greed	66. Striving
11. Pride	39. Obsessed	67. Blame
12. Judgment	40. Powerless	68. Disgraced
13. Indecisive	41. Anxious	69. Worthless
14. Selfish	42. Spiteful	70. Humiliated
15. Depressed	43. Lonely	71. Apathy
16. Demanding	44. Concerned	72. Hostile
17. Immoral	45. Dominated	73. Tolerate
18. Critical	46. Jealous	74. Blame
19. Resentment	47. Grudge	75. Defilement
20. Vulnerable	48. Argumentative	76. Degradation
21. Abandoned	49. Compulsive	77. Loss
22. Suspicious	50. Fighting	78. Poverty
23. Worry	51. Ruthless	79. Manipulated
24. Fear	52. Submissive	80. Demeaned
25. Dishonest	53. Inadequate	81. Humiliation
26. Doubt	54. Devastated	82. Controlled
27. Bored	55. Indifferent	83. Betrayed
28. Upset	56. Dread	84. Denial

SAMPLE EMOTIONS TO "STIR THE POT"		
POSITIVE EMOTIONS		
1. Love	29. Conscientious	57. Loyal
2. Joy	30. Devoted	58. Comfort
3. Peace	31. Satisfied	59. Reliable
4. Patient	32. Gratified	60. Truthful
5. Kind	33. Honest	61. Eager
6. Faithful	34. Happy	62. Excited
7. Goodness	35. Calm	63. Respect
8. Gentle	36. Adoring	64. Compassion
9. Self-Control	37. Amiable	65. Pleased
10. Passion	38. Agreeable	66. Encouraged
11. Stable	39. Compatible	67. Understood
12. Trust	40. Expectant	68. Dependable
13. Careful	41. Right	69. Desire
14. Harmonious	42. Composure	70. Curious
15. Warm	43. Dedicated	71. Empathy
16. Glad	44. Serenity	72. Recognized
17. Intimacy	45. Quiet	73. Exhilaration
18. Friendship	46. Consistent	74. Holy
19. Perfection	47. Content	75. Innocent
20. Elated	48. Enjoyment	76. Clarity
21. Grateful	49. Fulfilled	77. Security
22. Tranquility	50. Cherish	78. Abundance
23. Delight	51. Desire	79. Restored
24. Creative	52. Sensitive	80. Purity
25. Accepting/Accepted	53. Imaginative	81. Celebrated
26. Inspired	54. Enthusiastic	82. Flow
27. Hopeful	55. Agreeable	83. Believe
28. Unwavering	56. Blissful	84. Faith

Charts adapted in part from the book, *Feelings Buried Alive Never Die,* by Karol K. Truman

When you've identified your priorities, time frames, events, and emotions, identify and remove any interference between you and the innate healing potential that God created in you by applying the steps of the *Heart, Soul and Spirit Cleanse* from the previous chapters.

Don't forget the shortcut in Chapter 5!

FIVE Rules for the New You:

1. **SHOW UP.** Some authorities say that 90 percent of success is showing up...daily, hourly, to who you are and the purpose for which you were created, wherever you are, whatever you do, and whomever you're with. One motivational speaker says it this way: *"Be where you are, boy!"*

2. **PAY ATTENTION.** Listen for and obey the quiet but distinct voice in your spirit, leading you to take steps that, once taken, are followed by confirmation and blessing.

3. **SHARE YOUR TRUTH.** Don't withhold your wisdom or insight from others because of what they might think. Be what you believe; acting and speaking like God's ambassador wherever you go.

> When I was a teenager, my dad would remind me as I left the house, ***"Remember who you are and who you represent."***

4. **LET GO OF THE OUTCOME.** How people perceive you, how they treat you, whether they act or react to what you share, is up to them, not you. Your life is between you and God, not between you and other people.

Trying to make everything OK for other people will drag you, in the blink of an eye, into the cesspool that you just climbed out of, and that's no place for a child of God to live!

5. **Your Next Step:** You are not alone. Our mission is to deliver an easy to follow roadmap that supports your body, mind and spirit with direction, education and resources that you can easily master for life. We invite you to join our community of true health-seekers on **Facebook** who are creating lives of freedom, purpose, and joy.

 ## Nutshells and Takeaways from Chapter 10

FIVE Rules for the New You:

1. Show Up.
2. Pay Attention.
3. Share Your Truth.
4. Let Go of the Outcome.
5. You Are Not Alone.

Chapter 11

Healing is a Journey
and it's not always smooth sailing

This book was only hours away from going to press when we were reminded of a missing piece to the mystery of how healing happens. We've never addressed it before in any of our books, videos, seminars, or other materials: a phenomenon we call *"reactivation."*

You'll recognize what reactivation is and how it works when you combine what we've already discussed about memory, emotions, engrams, autopilot, and your body's survival priority. As someone dear to me said when I discussed *reactivation* with him, *"That explains a lot about my own behavior, and it could help thousands of people who don't understand why they can't seem to get a handle on some of their most troubling tendencies."*

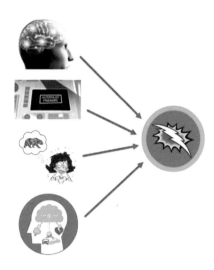

You see, healing is a journey that continues as long as you're alive. Just because symptoms disappear, life goes on and symptoms can reappear suddenly when stimuli are perceived subconsciously that are similar to those that started a condition. The resulting symptoms may feel more or less the same as when you first sought help.

> **Reactivation is actually a positive sign of ongoing healing that simply requires further attention.**

Why does reactivation happen?

Think of healing as a process that moves toward higher and higher levels in a spiral, rather than occurring along a straight line. Healing begins at one point on the spiral and as you progress, you wind around and around until you come to the same position as when you began, except that you're further up the spiral. Everything may look the same as it did further down; stimuli that were present at your starting point on the spiral are either present on the same point higher up, or your memory can even reconstruct them. Even though symptoms are likely to reappear, you're better and stronger than when you began.

Reactivation indicates that we are not completely OK with a past experience or relationship. We may acknowledge that it

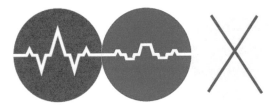

happened, but we are holding on to the possibility that it should *not* have happened or should have been different. *"It Happened,"* is a simple, statement of fact without qualifiers added.

How do you deal with reactivation?

The best way to handle a reactivation of physical symptoms is simply to repeat the processes you learned in the previous chapters. Remember to trust the process. There's no problem. You haven't lost ground; indeed, reactivation is evidence of the ground you've already gained and it's time to go deeper!

> The rule of thumb with reactivation is that it doesn't last long and if it happens again, the time will be shorter and symptoms will be milder; so, stay with your process!

Does healing eventually become permanent?

In our experience, physical healing can be truly lasting; but this depends on how you live your life in the eight areas that we listed in Chapter 2:

1. What you EAT
2. What you DRINK
3. What and How you BREATHE
4. How you EXERCISE (or don't!)
5. How you REST
6. What you THINK, FEEL, and BELIEVE
7. What you SPEAK
8. How you NURTURE YOUR SPIRIT

Every day is a new beginning. Healing is ongoing; it's as dynamic as each day is different. The better choices you make in each of the areas above, the healthier you'll be. It really is just that simple.

> Go to itsok.wholelifewholehealth.com to learn more about the
> *"Eight Master Keys that Unlock Your Total Health."*

What about Emotional Memory Engrams?

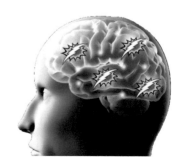

> Negative emotional memory engrams
> can reactivate
> just like physical symptoms.

Conscious memory sits like the visible part of an iceberg on the surface of our awareness. Subconscious memory, however, lies quietly under the surface, like the part of the iceberg we don't see; it's much larger and can be much more damaging if it's struck.

No experience can be put to rest while we continue to wish that it had not happened exactly as it did. Acceptance cannot succeed while resistance remains. We need to welcome – not run from – our worst memories and learn from them if we are to resolve them effectively. Gratitude is the ultimate goal of the *Heart, Soul and Spirit Cleanse.* When our gratitude for where we are and who we are today overwhelms the pain of past memory, we are free and we can live in victory.

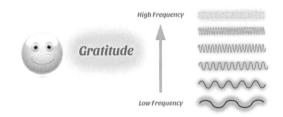

Experiences and relationships can be forgiven, but not forgotten ... not really.

Your brain catalogs and stores sights, sounds, smells, tastes, touches, temperature, lighting, humidity, and other physical aspects of experiences in exquisite detail. Your brain also cross-references and interlinks experiences, emotions, and physical responses that contain similar sensory information.

Remember the Reticular Activating System (RAS) and your body's autopilot that we discussed in Chapter 5? Reactivation can only occur when sensory stimuli during an experience – including the emotions before and during the experience – make it through your RAS, elicit a physical response (including hormones, such as adrenaline), and are recorded in subconscious memory for survival purposes when similar stimuli are present.

Reticular Activating System (RAS)

A woman experienced panic attacks in the middle of a grocery store. There seemed to be no rhyme or reason for these attacks, which could occur anywhere, anytime. Not knowing what caused the panic attacks and not wanting to risk setting one off, she was afraid to leave her house.

We worked together for several weeks, during which we identified and neutralized several emotional stimuli, using an energy-balancing process. The woman actually *forgot* about the panic attacks and, during a six-month re-evaluation, she said, *"If you had told me that I could feel this good this fast, I would not have believed you."*

She experienced a reactivation one day and returned to my office quite worried. I assured her that reactivation was normal and her system settled back down quickly. I saw her periodically for wellness visits over the course of at least three years, during which she experienced total freedom from the panic attacks that had once been debilitating.

The *real* power sources of negative engrams are ambushed *positive* emotions that we feel *prior* to a highly stressful experience. These positive emotions are virtually hidden from our ability to recall them, but they are deeply embedded into the incredibly complex memory traces that make up negative memory engrams.

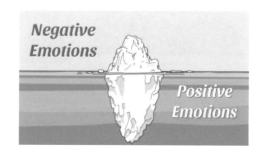

Reactivation is most likely to occur when an ambushed positive emotion is challenged in any way similar to a former experience stored in memory alongside highly charged negative emotions. The tsunami of emotions makes reactivation immune from reason.

A friend once asked, *"What do you do when you're coming from a place of love and helpfulness toward someone, but it isn't received that way?"* Whatever is in you that isn't healed from other experiences in which you felt unappreciated, or that your actions were discounted, makes you vulnerable to reactivation when anything similar happens.

The first instance, or insult, would have taken you by surprise and you would have felt ambushed. Your negative emotional memory engram was built out of every stimulus that your senses perceived. Reactivation is likely any time you are again demonstrating love and helpfulness, while hoping for a better response than before.

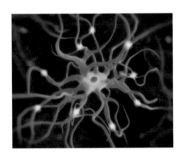

The comparisons that go on in your subconscious memory, as current stimuli are matched up with similar stimuli from past experiences, are as instantaneous and automatic as the responses they create. The question is what do you do?

First, master these four rules:

1. Show up
2. Pay attention
3. Share your truth
4. Let go of the outcome

Expect nothing from others. To the degree that you hope for or look for someone to recognize your actions toward them or on their behalf, you are setting yourself up for disappointment. Your actions are about you. Do what you do because that's who you are; how anyone else responds is about them; it's certainly not up to you.

When reactivation happens, look back through the most significant relationships you can recall and repeat the steps you learned in the *Heart, Soul and Spirit Cleanse*. No matter what the source of reactivation is, the process doesn't change.

If you have experiences that you feel less than happy about, pay attention, because reactivation of symptoms and/or emotions is likely to occur at some point. These experiences are not okay with you yet. There's no problem, but the healing process is just not complete.

> **When your gratitude for an experience is greater than you were ever wounded by it, you are free. Healing has succeeded and the likelihood of a reactivation is very small.**

"In everything give thanks; for this is God's will for you in Christ Jesus."
(1 Thessalonians 5:18, NASB)

Gratitude is always the shortest path. It is at the root of real, genuine, lasting healing. Gratitude has the ability to transform molecules. Dr. Candace Pert wrote about this in her book, *"Molecules of Emotion."* The emotion of gratitude, real heartfelt gratitude, for every experience that's ever occurred, no matter what, will transform molecules. Gratitude will change physiology (how your body functions) and it enables healing to occur at a rapid pace.

Gratitude won't change another person, by the way, so the people who don't appreciate you now probably won't appreciate you any better. It won't matter to you, however, because, as someone once said, *"You have to love people for who they are, not for who you want them to be."*

> **Emotional memory engrams are not subject to reason.**

Emotional memory engrams may be understandable, but they are in no way rational, and trying to reason with someone in the midst of a reactivating engram is futile.

A personal example that is very recent as of this writing is the best illustration I can imagine of emotional memory engram reactivation:

Barbara told me earlier in the day about driving past a house that she had contracted to purchase. A realty sign was out front and the driveway was full of cars. While that may not seem unusual, she had made a significant financial commitment,  having agreed together that this was her final home. We had enjoyed decorating and landscaping the new home as we looked at online pictures of the house and the grounds. The experience had been full of joy, expectation, creativity, and stability.

Barbara was shocked to see a "for sale" sign in the yard and cars in the driveway that was usually empty. When she told me about this, I wanted to get more information before drawing a potentially erroneous conclusion.

Later that evening, Barbara asked me to look at *another* house that she had found online in the same area.

Why not, right? A backup plan is not unreasonable.

Well, that isn't how I responded … not even close. I felt like I had been betrayed; that indeed, our marriage covenant had been violated, and that all we had agreed to and planned for was suddenly set ablaze! In a split second, my insides began churning uncontrollably with a gamut of emotions from shock to fury.

There was nothing I could do to stop the waves of emotion from turning me over and over like ocean waves that will drown you without a thought.

Barbara didn't understand my reaction. Nothing like this had ever happened throughout our marriage. I accused her of breaking faith and I told her that I felt lost, not being able to trust her after having agreed together on such a significant part of our journey. In fact, Barbara was *amused* by my response, and that just made the experience worse.

At one point during this exchange, which probably lasted about an hour, I said, "It's possible that I'm playing out a reactivation of the memory engram of when my first marriage exploded over the issue of infidelity."

"Wait," I said, *"This is also March at almost the exact time when my first wife and I separated."* That experience left me an emotional wreck that took months of work to repair.

Even though I could penetrate the swirl of emotions raging inside me enough to voice all this to Barbara, I still could not stop the tide. Stress hormones had already been unleashed and I would simply have to wait for them to dissipate. It was a miserable task to go to bed with the reactivated emotions still churning inside me. Praying through the "shortcut" in Chapter 5 was the only action that enabled me to sleep.

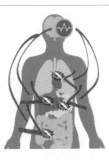

 I awoke the next morning with a clear understanding of what had happened. I asked Barbara to forgive me and we agreed that the phenomenon of reactivation, which has never before been written about in such detail, had to be added to this book.

We looked at the second house together, by the way, without difficulty. There was never really a problem between us; only the past rearing its ugly head, which we successfully decapitated.

Reactivation is instantaneous. Your brain compares incoming information with memories of other experiences, couples them with their associated emotions, and you're *off to the races* in a microsecond ... much faster than you can consciously gain control. The best you may be able to hope for is to remember that emotions are *"energy in motion"*: they will change if you simply wait them out.

Emotion: *"Energy in Motion"*

Many people find it helpful to use exercise to "burn off" the swell of adrenaline that reactivation creates. Physical activity and the deep breathing that accompanies it can help dissipate the flood of emotions.

Meanwhile, the *"Heart, Soul and Spirit Cleanse"* (or the shortcut in Chapter 5) can neutralize any negative emotional memory engram.

Other tools that we have found to be effective in helping to resolve a reactivation include ***"Belly Breathing"**** and the ***"Victory March."**** Both of these help you shift quickly from "emergency mode" into "healing mode." They take only minutes to perform and they're also helpful in relieving stress in the middle of a traffic jam, a heated discussion, or a conflict at work, when it's inconvenient to let off the steam another way.

*(Download the guides for these techniques from ItsOK.WholeLifeWholeHealth.com.)

If you express the emotions that can hit like a tsunami, as I did in the story above, you risk laying waste to others around you who may be entirely innocent. Cleaning up the mess in the aftermath can take a long time and leave lasting scars.

Reactivation may occur in degrees, from mild to severe, when experiences contain aspects even remotely similar to ones stored as negative emotional memory engrams. Generally, the more aspects of a current experience or relationship that can be compared to one stored as a negative engram, the greater the degree of reactivation. In a strange paradox, however, the most severe reactivations may occur with only a hint of similarity to a previously stored experience.

This is the nature of survival responses: They can be overblown, because, after all, the body does not think, judge or reason, it responds for survival alone.

All of our discussion so far has centered on *negative* emotional memory, but everything applies equally to *positive* engrams. For example, this book is being written in the spring, which is one of my favorite times of year.

I awoke early one morning a few weeks ago to the sound of song birds that are absent during winter. I thought, *"Oh, spring is here!"* Perhaps two weeks later, the earliest blooms began to appear on a few trees, and as soon as we could open the windows, a fresh breeze wiped away the stale winter air of a closed house. Every spring feels the same, including a freshly invigorated sense of new life and energy. Such is the physical picture painted vividly in my memory, along with renewed feelings of joy and anticipation.

What is your favorite season? What are the feelings you associate with it? Favorite seasons and holiday celebrations are examples of your own positive emotional memory engrams that reactivate every year. The truth is, we don't spend enough time or energy cultivating positive memories. More often, we just feel lucky to have some.

From Claudia Gabrielle, MD:

"This stuff really works! I say a prayer thanking God for all I took away from a 23-year experience, instead of going into a deep hole of bitterness every time I pass a sign or a building that reminds me of it. It has taken years of repeating aloud, *'Thank you, God, for what I learned, what I am learning, and what I will learn.'* I've done the Belly Breathing and the Victory March daily for the last 7 years and the *Heart, Soul and Spirit Cleanse* every 1-2 weeks for 10 years. The change has become cellular and I am so grateful for where I am today and who I have become that I wouldn't trade it for anything! Romans 8:28 is so true, *'God is working it all out for the good of those who love Him.'*"

Negative emotions connected to experiences seemingly long "forgotten" can come like a flood that bursts a dam and seems to wash away all the healing progress we've made.

If reactivation happens, remember that it's *evidence* of healing and a part of the healing process that simply requires more attention.

Resisting a reactivation is virtually impossible. Its force need not carry you away, even though you might have felt like a victim when the original insult occurred. Use what you've learned in this book and celebrate your victories every day!

Let go of your "Balloons and Butterflies"

For profound and lasting healing to take root, progress unhindered, and succeed fully, we have to be willing to let go of what we call our *"balloons and butterflies."* These are the stories we tell ourselves and others about experiences that we wish hadn't happened or wish had been different.

Our stories are full of details about what, where, when, why, and how an experience happened. The story may contain elements of truth, but we usually embellish or modify our narratives with *balloons and butterflies* to make us feel better about ourselves and look good to others.

We are often the victims in our stories. *Balloons and butterflies* are really no more than lies in which we blame others rather than humble ourselves and take responsibility for our own words and actions. We make ourselves into perpetual victims and, as such, we are bound to repeat history over and over.

As victims, we cannot learn what we need to learn and we prevent lasting healing. Our subconscious, however, stores information accurately, so, our *balloons and butterflies* serve only to make us extra vulnerable to negative engram reactivation.

> **The truth is that we are all where our choices have led us.**

Barbara dissolves any sense of condemnation that people often feel about their worst memories with a simple principle that she learned during her time in the ministry:

> *"God took you a way you wouldn't have gone*
> *to teach you what you needed to learn.*
> *It was all for your training."*

You can set yourself free from the wounds of past memory whenever you're ready. When you are truly grateful for your experiences and relationships, you won't need *balloons and butterflies* to make you feel better about yourself or look good to others.

After all, *It Happened, It's Over,* and *It's OK Now.*

Nutshells and Takeaways from Chapter 11

- Healing is a journey that continues as long as you're alive.

- Reactivation is actually a positive sign of ongoing healing that simply requires further attention.

- Healing is a process that moves upward toward higher and higher levels in a spiral, rather than occurring along a straight line.

- Remember to trust the process.

- Reactivation doesn't last long and if it happens again, the time will be shorter and symptoms will be less and less severe.

- Healing is ongoing; it's as dynamic as each day is different.

- Experiences and relationships can be forgiven, but rarely forgotten.

- The *real* power sources of negative engrams are ambushed *positive* emotions that we feel *prior* to a highly stressful experience.

- Negative emotional memory engrams can reactivate, just like physical symptoms.

- Emotional memory engrams are not subject to reason.

- Emotional memory engrams may be understandable, but they are in no way rational.

- Reactivation is instantaneous.

- Emotions are *"energy in motion"*: they will change if you simply wait them out.

- Physical activity and the deep breathing that accompanies it can help dissipate the flood of emotions.

- The *"Heart, Soul and Spirit Cleanse"* (or the shortcut in Chapter 5) can neutralize the negative emotional memory engram.

- Expressing emotions that can hit like a tsunami risks laying waste to others around you who may be entirely innocent. Cleaning up the mess in the aftermath can take a long time and leave lasting scars.

- Reactivation may occur in degrees, from mild to severe.

- The most severe reactivations may occur with only a hint of similarity to an experience stored as a negative emotional memory engram.

- No experience can be put to rest while we continue to wish that it had not happened exactly as it did.

- Acceptance cannot succeed while resistance remains.

- When our gratitude for where we are and who we are today overwhelms the pain of past memory, we are free and we can live in victory.

- Whatever in you isn't healed from other experiences makes you vulnerable to reactivation when anything similar happens.

- Master these four rules:
  1. Show up
  2. Pay attention
  3. Share your truth
  4. Let go of the outcome

- Expect nothing from others.

- Your actions are about you. How anyone else responds is about them; it's certainly not up to you.

- If you have experiences that you feel less than happy about, reactivation of symptoms and/or emotions is likely to occur.

- When your gratitude for an experience is greater than you were ever wounded by it, you are free.

- *"In everything give thanks; for this is God's will for you in Christ Jesus."* (1 Thessalonians 5:18, NASB)

- Gratitude is always the shortest path. It is at the root of real, genuine, lasting healing.

- Gratitude has the ability to transform molecules.

- Gratitude will change physiology (how your body functions) and it enables healing to occur at a rapid pace.

- Your gratitude won't change another person.

- *"You have to love people for who they are, not for who you want them to be."*

- *Balloons and butterflies* are lies that we tell ourselves about experiences and relationships that we wish hadn't happened or wish had been different.

- *"God took you a way you wouldn't have gone to teach you what you needed to learn. It was all for your training."*

Your body responds according to its *design*,
not your *desire*.

Chapter 12

The Heart of the Matter

Healing is sometimes compared to peeling away the layers of an onion, but we've never liked that analogy. Have you ever peeled an onion all the way? The layers are a major pain to separate and by the time you're finished, there's nothing remaining. You're left with tears streaming down your face and a pile of garbage!

Artichokes, Not Onions

We prefer to compare healing to peeling away the layers of an artichoke. The layers are easy to grasp, although the leaves of a raw artichoke have tiny points on their tips that hurt when you peel the leaves away, much like the often sharp pain of finding your own "layers."

Unlike the emptiness of peeling away the layers of an onion, peeling the leaves of an artichoke reveals its heart and makes it worth the effort.

Healing is like peeling away the layers of an artichoke: You get to the heart.

When you've mastered the steps of the *Heart, Soul and Spirit Cleanse,* you will have achieved victory in virtually every area of your life, because, as you've learned by now, true healing occurs in your spirit, soul (or mind), and body.

Victory is a word that is almost never used in casual conversation, but it applies to the processes and principles that we've shared throughout this book. According to Merriam-Webster's online dictionary, victory is the *"achievement of mastery or success in a struggle or endeavor against odds or difficulties."* Victory is not an unending process, like peeling an onion. Victory is an achievement, like reaching the heart of an artichoke.

Every healing you experience is a victory, whether it's physical, mental, emotional, or spiritual.

We pray that this book empowers you to move from victory to victory in every area of your life.

An old man once built a bridge across the river that separated his village from others nearby. He cut down trees from the forest on one side of the river, dragged the logs one-by-one to the shoreline and anchored them high enough from the water to allow for monsoon rains that would swell the

river every year. He tied the logs together tightly and added a railing. After making sure that the bridge was safe to cross, the old man sat down to admire his work.

A young man passed by who had seen the old man working on his bridge. He said, *"Old man, you've lived by this river your whole life. You know every rock in it and where to step to reach the other shore in any season, wet or dry. Why in the world did you build a bridge?"*

The old man, still gazing at his finished bridge, said simply, *"Young man, I didn't build this bridge for me. I built it for those who come after me."*

This book is a bridge that we didn't write for us, but for you and others who will come after us. It isn't enough that we know where very rock in the river is and how to cross it in any season. This bridge enables you to cross the river safely, even when the waters of your life are raging.

No More Problems

When Barbara turned 60 years-old, she decided that she wouldn't have any more problems in her life. *"I'm too old for problems,"* she declared. *"Problems take agreement. No one can make me play stupid games without my permission and any game is over when someone quits playing."*

How do you rule out problems when you don't control the world or the people in it? Seems impossible, and yet, Barbara has succeeded in living in what we call, the *"Realm of the Miraculous,"* in which problems are exceedingly rare.

One of Barbara's *"plumb lines"* that she lives by is a Scripture from Proverbs 10:22:

> **"It is the blessing of the Lord that makes rich, and He adds no sorrow to it."** (NASB)

The Scripture above is more than just a religious concept or philosophy. It describes a literal, spiritual realm in which problem-centered emotions like *worry, fear,* and *doubt,* are overwhelmed and replaced by *trust, confidence,* and *gratitude.* The former emotions provide an environment for problems to thrive, while the latter emotions foster an environment characterized by a continual sense of peace.

Worry
Fear
Doubt

Trust
Confidence
Gratitude

The obvious question is, *"What or whom are we trusting?"* The answer is contained in the Scripture: ***"the Lord."***

Proverbs 10:22 and countless other Scriptures invite us to trust our Creator to direct our steps and provide for every aspect of our lives. That's just totally unrealistic, though, isn't it? After all, the idea flies in the face of reason. All our training, from earliest childhood on, about self-determination and self-sufficiency, allows no room for what rational people might call a fantasy. So, instead, most people strive and drive in a realm fraught with problems of every description, from simple stress to illness and bad marriages that take an enormous toll.

> More people *read* the Scriptures than *apply* them.

What if it were possible for you to make the same determination that Barbara did when she turned 60? What if living in the *Realm of the Miraculous* is as real as the words on this page, and all you have to do to enter a realm beyond problems is trust the One Who created you and everything else? Isn't that worth the risk, or at least a look?

At one time in our history, people *depended* on the *Realm of the Miraculous* for virtually everything good in their lives, including health, wealth, and even their form of government. Self-determination got the ancient Israelites in trouble every time they tried it, but

when they trusted God and followed His directions, the people prospered.

God is no less faithful today than He was thousands of years ago to provide, miraculously, sovereignly, for every aspect of your life. The means of living in His provision are the same: Trust Him entirely and follow His direction. Only then can you discover the *Realm of the*

Miraculous, in which all hurts are healed, all needs are met, and there is nothing as low as a problem. In such a realm, you make nothing happen out of the strength of your own will; instead, you subject your will to the One Who said, *"Let there be you."*

> *"Living by faith,"* taking every step by God's personal direction
> may be uncommon, but the *Realm of the Miraculous*
> is still available to anyone who chooses it.

A four-step pattern that runs throughout the Scriptures provides some insight into what trusting God looks like:

> Revelation, when met with obedience, is followed swiftly
> by confirmation, and then the blessing flows.

1. **Revelation** is the direction that God indicates.

2. **Obedience** is following His direction by taking the step(s) you are shown.

3. **Confirmation** always follows obedience and may be seen within a few minutes to a few days; it's evidence that you accurately interpreted the revelation and took the appropriate action(s).

4. **Blessing** flows over time as trust between you and God grows.

> The four-step cycle of *Revelation-Obedience-Confirmation-Blessing* hinges on obedience. Forward progress stops abruptly when revelation is not met with obedience.

Faith means *trust*, in Hebrew, and throughout the Scriptures, God demonstrates that He honors faith. He honors being trusted and, while it may not be an easy lesson, living in His peace, provision, purpose, protection and presence is marvelous beyond words.

> *"You have searched me, Lord, and You know me.*
> *You know when I sit and when I rise;*
> *You perceive my thoughts from afar.*
> *You discern my going out and my lying down;*
> *You are familiar with all my ways.*
> *Before a word is on my tongue You, Lord, know it completely.*
> *You hem me in behind and before, and You lay Your hand upon me.*
> *Marvelous is such knowledge beyond me;*
> *It is impregnable; I cannot reach to it."*
> (Psalm 139:1-6, CLV)

You may well find it hard to wrap your brain around a literal, practical relationship with your Creator in which He provides and directs every aspect of your life. We can assure you, however, such a relationship is utterly simple, its rewards are incomparable, and it removes you from the usual human stresses of striving and driving.

Barbara has not drawn a paycheck in almost 30 years since leaving her athletic apparel stores. I have not drawn one since I left my wellness practice at the end of January, 2009. In all the time since, we have witnessed God's

miraculous engineering of relationships and situations that have provided abundantly for our every need and more, exactly as the Scriptures promise:

> *"Now my God shall be filling your every need in accord with His riches in glory in Christ Jesus."* (Philippians 4:19)

We've lived in wonderful homes and in a kind of peace and joy that others have envied, tried to emulate, and that most have found hard to comprehend.

We offer no boast in any of this that we've shared above. We simply offer a modern testimony to ancient Scriptural principles that operate today as much as when they were first written. Only modern beliefs and traditions – like those of a flat Earth – make them unavailable or seemingly unattainable to our "sophisticated" minds.

Consider again what was written in the Introduction to this book:

> In his book, *Learned Optimism*, psychologist, Martin Seligman, wrote that, *"humans believe that what they think is true, simply because they think it."* What you think or believe may not be true at all, but what *is* true remains true no matter what you think or believe.

If you've had trouble believing that what we've written could apply to you in your life today, we get it. Resistance to change is normal and is increased when current beliefs are challenged.

> **God is a gentleman.**
> **He won't crash through a closed door.**
> **The door knob is on the inside.**

> *"Behold, I stand at the door and knock; if anyone hears My voice and opens the door, I will come in to him and will dine with him, and he with Me."*
> (Revelation 3:20, NASB)

Barbara's prayer is this: *"I pray that the hidden things come to light and what's not of God is exposed and removed. I pray for His strategy for the victory, for Heaven's View in this and every situation. I pray that God shut the doors no man can open for your protection and blow the doors off the hinges for your new beginning."*

Keep your hands off the door knobs and simply ask, *"Father, what would You have me do?"* Wait for an answer. Do nothing out of desperation.

Most people have heard the Scripture, ***"Be still and know that I am God"*** (Psalm 46:10, NIV). In Hebrew, however, it reads, ***"RELAX and know that I am God."*** Comforting, isn't it?

What if all this is true? What would that look like in your life?

By August, 2007, I had engaged business coaches and life coaches, but when I asked Barbara to be my spiritual coach, she gave me one assignment: *"Read the book and do what it says."* Her "book" was the Bible, but this wasn't the answer I wanted, so her counsel meant little to me at the time.

Then, she turned me on to the *Daily Bible in Chronological Order*, by F. Lagard Smith (see Recommended Reading). By the time I began reading it for the *second* time, I saw patterns, precedents and principles that operate in our lives today. It became apparent that, while our bodies behave according to scientific principles, they respond reliably to how we follow or violate scriptural instructions.

I also saw God's personality. I discovered what He valued, the extent of His patience, and what He tolerated versus what He didn't. I saw how His instructions produced the results He promised when they were followed and when they weren't, and people reaped the consequences of their actions either way.

Moses establishes the Blessing and the Curse
(Deuteronomy 11:26-28)

> *"I am setting before you today a blessing and a curse – the blessing if you obey the commands of the Lord your God that I am giving you today; the curse if you disobey the commands of the Lord your God."* (Deuteronomy 11:26-28)

Scriptural principles are scientifically demonstrable. When Jesus instructed His disciples to, *"Seek first the kingdom and its righteousness, and these all shall be added to you"* (Mathew 6:33, CLNT), He had already provided examples and comparisons to illustrate the Father's trustworthiness to provide our needs:

> *Do not worry about your life, what you will eat or drink; or about your body, what you will wear. Is not life more than food, and the body more than clothes? Look at the birds of the air; they do not sow or reap or store away in barns, and yet your heavenly Father feeds them. Are you not much more valuable than they? Can any one of you by worrying add a single hour to your life?*

> *And why do you worry about clothes? See how the flowers of the field grow. They do not labor or spin. Yet I tell you that not even Solomon in all his splendor was dressed like one of these. If that is how God clothes the grass of the field, which is here today and tomorrow is thrown into the fire, will He not much more clothe you – you of little faith? So do not worry, saying, "What shall we eat?" or, "What shall we drink?" or, "What shall we wear?" For the [nations] run after all these things, and your heavenly Father knows that you need them. But seek first His kingdom and His righteousness, and all these things will be given to you as well. Therefore do not worry about tomorrow, for tomorrow will worry about itself. Each day has enough trouble of its own.* (Mathew 6:25-34, NIV)

Barbara calls the Bible the *"Basic Instructions Before Leaving Earth."* The passage above is a good example of this, because the key to understanding why most people have such a hard time believing the Scriptures and living in the *Realm of the Miraculous* is two-fold, and hidden in plain sight in the text above:

1. *"You of little Faith."* It's no wonder that most people are caught up in striving and driving, pushing and shoving to survive, always seeking more, better, and faster. They trust God so little that their efforts to *play* God crowd Him out. He certainly *could* overpower them, but He won't impose His will on someone who doesn't trust Him ... at least not now.

God's provision will trump ours when we stop acting out of our own will and self-interest, and trust Him entirely.

2. **"But seek first His kingdom and His righteousness, and all these things will be given to you as well."** This is one of many *"If, then"* statements found throughout the Scriptures: *"If you do this, then this will happen."* In this statement, we discover that

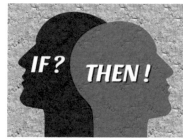

God's provision is conditioned on our posture toward Him. If we seek Him *first*, rather than rely on our own wits and will, He provides what we need (and more). If not, we're on our own.

Self-reliance, self-will, and self-determination is the condition that probably describes most people you know – certainly most people you pass on the way to work every day. They consider it normal to virtually wear themselves out with stress, worry and striving. The doctors' offices and hospitals are full of people who have exhausted their bodies, minds, and spirits to the point that medication, surgery, and radiation is required just to prop them up. How sad and how

unnecessary, when a far better way lies in front of our faces, and all that is required is faith, or trust in the One Who created us in the first place and said, **"It is good."** Perhaps we ought to take Him at His word.

I confess that I knew none of this in a practical way when Barbara, as my Spiritual coach in 2007, said, *"Read the book and do what it says."* Over the course of several years, however, I discovered that the Scriptures are literally alive and all the principles they contain are operating now, just like the law of gravity, whether we believe them or not.

> *"The word of God is living and active and sharper than any two-edged sword, and piercing as far as the division of soul and spirit, of both joints and marrow, and able to judge the thoughts and intentions of the heart."* (Hebrews 4:12, NASB)

The daily reality of living in and walking out the instructions contained in the Scriptures on a daily basis is a far better, and far richer experience than I could have imagined. Barbara and I would wish this for you too. For all that we've learned about how to help people restore and sustain their health, spiritual well-being is found in the words written in a book that has survived millennia. The Bible is no longer listed in the top 10 best sellers, because it outsells all other books every year!

Isn't it time to live in the peace and presence of God until you meet Him face to face? I know no better guide than Barbara Brown. She lives in the *Realm of the Miraculous* and she knows how to bring others there too.

To continue your journey, go to <u>BarbaraBrown.com</u>. Take advantage of *"Morning Magicals," "Light Up the Scriptures," "Barbara's World,"* and keep a sharp eye out for more programs to come.

Until then . . .

> *The Lord bless you and keep you;*
> *The Lord make His face shine on you*
> *and be gracious to you;*
> *The Lord turn His face toward you*
> *and give you peace.*
>
> (Numbers 6:24-26, NIV)

Nutshells and Takeaways from Chapter 12

- Healing is like peeling away the layers of an artichoke: You get to the heart.

- Every healing you experience is a victory, whether it's physical, mental, emotional, or spiritual.

- The *Realm of the Miraculous* is one in which problems are exceedingly rare.

- This is an important plumb line for your life: ***"It is the blessing of the Lord that makes rich, and He adds no sorrow to it"*** (Proverbs 10:22, NASB).

- The *Realm of the Miraculous* is one in which problem-centered emotions like *worry*, *fear*, and *doubt*, are overwhelmed and replaced by *trust, confidence,* and *gratitude.*

- If living in a realm above problems is as simple as trusting the One Who created you and everything else, isn't it worth the risk, or at least a look?

- The *Realm of the Miraculous* is one in which all hurts are healed, all needs are met, and there is nothing as low as a problem.

- *"Living by faith,"* taking every step by God's personal direction may be uncommon, but the *Realm of the Miraculous* is available to anyone who chooses it.

- A four-step pattern that runs throughout the Scriptures provides some insight into what trusting God looks like:

  1. **Revelation** – the direction that God indicates in your spirit
  2. **Obedience** – following God's direction by taking the step(s) you're shown
  3. **Confirmation** – may be seen within minutes to a few days following your obedience to God's revelation
  4. **Blessing** – flows over time as trust between you and God grows

- The four-step cycle of *Revelation-Obedience-Confirmation-Blessing* hinges on obedience and stops abruptly when obedience does not follow revelation.

- Faith means *trust*, in Hebrew and God honors faith. He is trustworthy and He honors being trusted.

- Only modern beliefs, traditions, and our "sophisticated" minds make living by faith and living in the *Realm of the Miraculous* appear unavailable or seemingly unattainable.

- Psychologist, Martin Seligman, wrote that, *"humans believe that what they think is true, simply because they think it."* What you think or believe may not be true at all, but what *is* true remains true no matter what you think or believe.

- Resistance to change is normal and is increased when current beliefs are challenged.

- God is a gentleman. He won't crash through a closed door. The door knob is on the inside.

- Simply ask, *"Father, what would You have me do?"* Wait for an answer. Do nothing out of desperation.

- Barbara advises, *"Read the book [the Bible] and do what it says."* She calls the Bible the *"Basic Instructions Before Leaving Earth."*

- While our bodies behave according to scientific principles, they respond reliably to how we follow or violate scriptural instructions.

- Scriptural principles are scientifically demonstrable.

- Most people are caught up in striving and driving, pushing and shoving to survive, always seeking more, better, and faster. They trust God so little that their efforts to *play* God crowd Him out.

- God's provision will trump ours when we stop acting out of our own will and self-interest, and trust Him entirely.

- ***"But seek first His kingdom and His righteousness, and all these*** *things will be given to you as well"* is one of many *"If, then"* statements found throughout the Scriptures.

- If we seek Him *first*, rather than rely on our own wits and will, He provides what we need (and more). If not, we're on our own.

- Self-reliance, self-will, and self-determination are conditions that probably describe most people you know.

- Isn't it time to live in the peace and presence of God until you meet Him face to face? Go to **www.BarbaraBrown.com**. Take advantage of *"Morning Magicals," "Light Up the Scriptures," "Barbara's World,"* and keep a sharp eye out for more programs to come.

Recommended Reading

See ItsOK.WholeLifeWholeHealth.com for direct links to these resources.

- *The Daily Bible in Chronological Order*, New International Version, F. LaGard Smith
- *The Biology of Belief*, Bruce Lipton, Ph.D.
- *Feelings Buried Alive Never Die*, Karol K. Truman
- *Happiness Is a Choice*, Barry Neil Kaufman, Ph.D.
- *The Field*, Lynne McTaggart
- *Learned Optimism*, Martin Seligman, Ph.D.
- *Infinite Mind*, Valerie V. Hunt, Ed.D.

Other Books by Barbara Brown, MSE, and Dr. Tom Taylor

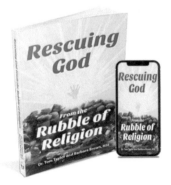

About the Authors

Barbara Brown, MSE, is a walking miracle, being divinely healed of muscular dystrophy. She has been the guest of kings and presidents, bringing the *Realm of the Miraculous* and imparting Whole Life and Whole Health to palaces and boardrooms around the world.

When Barbara nearly died from a ruptured appendix, the experience compelled her to take personal responsibility for her health and sent her on a quest for solutions that work 100% of the time.

With three Masters Degrees in science and education, Barbara is an author, ordained minister, businesswoman, speaker, and wellness advocate, helping people from the whorehouse to the White House re-awaken and restore their original design, and fulfill the purpose for which they were created.

Barbara is the author of a three-part book series, titled, ***GOD is GOD and We Are Not***. She is also the co-author of the books, ***Your Personal Roadmap to Whole Body Cleansing*** and ***Miracles with Minerals***.

Learn more about Barbara at **BarbaraBrown.com**.

Dr. Tom Taylor is recognized internationally as an expert in bio-energetics and practical nutrition, focusing on solutions that help restore, sustain, and improve health and well-being 100% of the time. *"Anything less,"* he says, *"means you are someone's science experiment."*

He has trained chiropractors and other health care practitioners from around the world, written dozens of professional articles for a worldwide practitioner network, and led seminars for the public all over the U.S., teaching principles and processes of how to "Live the Victory" in every area of life.

Dr. Taylor's other books include the **Nutrition Success Manual** for health care practitioners and a unique examination of the Scriptures, titled, **Rescuing God From the Rubble of Religion.** He is also the co-author of **Your Personal Roadmap to Whole Body Cleansing** and **Miracles with Minerals**.

Learn more about Dr. Taylor at **WholeLifeWholeHealth.com**.

> **Take advantage of all the online resources for this book at ItsOK.WholeLifeWholeHealth.com**

Divine Health is Your Original Design

Learn more:

www.**WholeLifeWholeHealth**.com

Made in the USA
Columbia, SC
29 October 2023

25008640R00095